WESTMIN

A Survey of Three States in the 1980s

Editor:

Allan Peachment

The Federation Press

1995

Published in Sydney by

The Federation Press
PO Box 45, Annandale, NSW, 2038.
3/56-72 John St, Leichhardt, NSW, 2040.
Ph (02) 552 2200. Fax (02) 552 1681.

National Library of Australia
Cataloguing-in-Publication entry

Westminister Inc. : a survey of three states in the eighties.

Includes index.
ISBN 1 86287 164 7.

1. Western Australia – Politics and government – 1976-1990
2. Western Australia – Economic conditions – 1976-1990.
3. South Australia – Politics and government – 1976-1990
4. South Australia – Economic conditions – 1976-1990
5. Victoria – Politics and government – 1976-1990
6. Victoria – economic conditions – 1976-1990. I.
Peachment, A.

320.994

Typeset by The Federation Press, Leichhardt, NSW.
Printed by Ligare Pty Ltd, Riverwood, NSW.

Contents

Dedicated to
Genevieve, Hetty and Milly

Contributors – Biographical Details

Jean Holmes, formerly a Reader and Senior Associate in the Department of Political science at the University of Melbourne, taught Australian politics there for more than 20 years. Her publications include *The Government of Victoria*, and *The Australian Federal System* and more than a hundred articles on all aspects of State and federal politics. She has also taught courses in Australian politics at Harvard University and Pennsylvania State University in the United States, and presented papers at international political science conferences on many occasions. A regular media commentator on Victorian politics on radio and television, Jean Holmes has always had a keen eye for the crotchets of political life and an awareness of the importance of the structures of government for the health of a democratic polity.

Allan Peachment has a PhD in Comparative Politics and holds research degrees in Australian Federalism and Comparative Government and has published in the fields of Australian federalism, policy experimentation, science and public policy, education and training, ethics and business/government relations. He was senior vice president of the Royal Institute of Public Administration of Australia (WA Division) and in 1989 was made a National fellow. He has delivered invited papers to a number of international conferences, and for a time was principle consultant to the Indonesian Government (*Lembaga Administrasi Negara*) and to the Indonesian Institute of Sciences (*Papitek Lipi*) Centre for the Analysis of Science and Technology Development. Allan is Associate Professor in Public Administration in the School of Management and Marketing at Curtin University, Perth, Western Australia.

Ian Radbone has a Phd in History and has taught government-related subjects for 18 years. He is now a senior lecturer at the International Graduate School of Management, University of South Australia. He has also worked within the public services of both the Commonwealth and South Australian governments and is currently an adviser to South Australia's newly established Passenger Transport Board. Ian Radbone has published widely in the areas of public administration and transport policy and was for most of the 1980s the chronicler of South Australia's administrative developments for the Australian Journal of Public Administration. He is currently a member of that journal's editorial board.

Preface

The Australian States are notoriously parochial – particularly in matters political. The Canberra scene aside, only when some dramatic event occurs in one State or another (but usually in New South Wales or Victoria) is it reported nationally, and then with a 24-hour media life-span. Whether this is a weakness in the media, a result of our federal diversity or a version of the "tyranny of distance" is debatable. In fact, such parochialism probably occurs in parts of the world where you would least expect it. As an American friend once said, "if you really want to witness parochialism, come to New York, there it is an art form".

Whatever the case it is frequently easier to acquire an understanding of political events occurring overseas than it is for those who live in one Australian State to follow political developments in another. For example, in Western Australia there was massive and sophisticated media coverage of the royal commission into *WA Inc*; more so than any other single event in the State's history. This was accompanied by much analysis and "spin doctoring" – where party spokespersons help promote politically favourable interpretations of events to journalists. However, there was almost no worthwhile media coverage of comparable events occurring in other States. I presume that a similar situation to this was occurring to those living in other parts of Australia in relation to what was happening in the West, but I cannot be sure.

This limiting parochialism was turned to advantage by providing the main driving force for this book. As one who teaches comparative public administration, I held the not unusual view that only a comparative treatment of the *WA Inc* debacle, with what appeared from a distance to be comparable circumstances in both Victoria and South Australia, would allow better informed judgements to be made on all three States. Despite this expectation, and with a little pre-reading on both States, my first reading of the chapters by my co-writers caught me quite unprepared; the circumstances they described for their respective States produced a combination of shock, disbelief and astonishment! While parliamentary accountability had obviously suffered in all three States, it had done so for mainly different reasons. More commonly, not only was the Victorian experience of financial trauma different from the South Australian, but each differed from the *WA Inc* experience. Yet all three cases took place concurrently within the same federal system! I am unable to judge if those who live in other States will be equally surprised at the details of the *WA Inc* experience.

If the Western Australian experience is any guide, the lack of information on the financial and political disasters in other States allowed distorted and negative explanations to be made of the causes and consequences of *WA Inc*. West Australians, for example, were told that because of the *WA Inc* debacle the State was now a kind of pariah and that international capital would be wary about investing here. Of course, in the circumstances one would expect the State's international credit rating to dip, for a number of budget-related reasons, but there was little mention in this State of the often worse circumstances in other States. Indeed, in other parts of the world, staggering financial losses had been incurred, not only in the public sector but in the private sector also. In the 1980s both government and business corruption had been widespread it would seem. The idea that market forces related to investment may impact negatively on Western Australia, more so than on Victoria and South Australia for example, simply did not make sense. Of course, in making their investment decisions, multinational corporations took account of a much wider picture than merely West Australian anguish at its recent history. In a related vein, it is also hoped that the book will give the lie to the now expressed "official" view that *WA Inc* had nothing to do with a failure of the processes of parliament or the relationship between the political party in power at the time and some senior echelons of the public service. Nothing could be further from the truth.

The book took much longer to complete than was originally planned and I take this opportunity to thank my co-writers, Jean Holmes and Ian Radbone, for their patience. The delay has not been to the book's disadvantage however as, in each State, new events kept unfolding and it seemed there would be no end to the fall-out from the various royal commissions and other inquiries.

I thank Chris Holt, Kathy Fitzhenry and Liz Halley of The Federation Press for their advice and tireless assistance at all times. I also acknowledge Curtin University for the privileges it provides, in particular a working environment in which important research and publication is highly valued.

Allan Peachment
Curtin University of Technology
PERTH
January 1995

1

Victoria:

State Enterprise and Labor in the Eighties

Jean Holmes

Historical residues

The Australian State was activist and interventionist from the outset. Our first colonies were State settlements, ruled by governors whose duty it was to establish a European model of society in an unknown continent, and in due course develop a suitable economic system for its support. Our colonial legacy is one of pervasive State intervention and a political experience that takes for granted the pattern of activist governments geared to mobilising public resources to meet the demands of unions, farmers' associations, consumers, business groups, and so on, without end.[1]

With the granting of self-government to the colonies in the 1850s the first Westminster model colonial parliaments were set up. In Victoria the prevailing radical democratic climate was such that most of the emphasis was placed on the representative system when the Constitution was drawn up, and often existing administrative arrangements were left untouched. (Holmes 1980, 340-351) For example, the practice of giving public officials their own statutory powers was continued, allowing the newly formed democratic parliaments to move rapidly into large-scale development projects – railway construction, irrigation schemes, ports and

1 Irrigation schemes supplying free water so that farming settlements could establish themselves were typical of these early alliances. See also Miller JDB and Jinks B, *Australian Government and Politics*, 4th ed, Duckworth London, 1970, 115ff, for other illustrations.

harbours – as they sought to meet the demands flowing through the adult franchise representative system. State-organised activity was responsible for public investment rising to 30-40 per cent of total investment in Australia in the 1870s and 1880s, a percentage that was to be maintained for more than 100 years (Spann et al 1973, 89).

Thus we have no true "laisser faire" past, no tradition of small responsive government geared primarily to the demands of individual entrepreneurs. The pattern that was established early in Australia's political and economic history was one of coalition between governments and developers, a legacy of "statism" that shapes the machinery of Australian government still. The developer role is taken for granted by today's interventionist States, actively underwriting social and economic development through joint ventures, subsidies for industries, overseas promotions, the provision of infrastructure and so on. The links between the State and business and labour and the blurring of private/public boundaries in Australian society set the parameters that govern the political and public administration processes in State and federal government in Australia today.

Victorian governments have been particularly innovative in devising administrative structures that allowed them to intervene in the State economy and conduct business enterprises away from the political limelight. Incorporated authorities were first set up in Victoria to avoid the evils of political patronage characteristic of the factional politics of the 19th century, particularly in the Railways Department where the minister shared his responsibility with an independent board.

By 1902 Victoria was still suffering from the effects of the 1890s economic depression and from a corresponding decline in population. In an effort to revitalise the State's economy, the Liberal premier, Sir William Irvine, decided to launch a series of developmental projects in irrigation, water supply and land settlement. He took the New Zealand public corporation as his administrative model for restoring economic prosperity to the State, and set up a number of financially and administratively independent public enterprises outside direct ministerial control. Described as "the golden age of socialism" but a "socialism sans doctrines", it was an interventionist strategy that provided a profitable environment for private enterprise within Victoria, while avoiding political conflict with the business interests important to the Liberal party.

The rise and fall of the public corporation in Victoria

For the next two decades, the provision of public services requiring technical expertise was handed over to the new public statutory corporations with a will. Victorian governments (socialist and non-socialist in intent) went on to use various forms of incorporated agencies to expand government intervention indiscriminately for the next 50 years. Ultimately Victorian public corporations were to be responsible for more than two-thirds of all public expenditure in the State, and for the employment of the bulk of the public sector workforce. Corporations such as the now disbanded State Electricity Commission of Victoria and the Melbourne and Metropolitan Board of Works were among Australia's largest enterprises. Their impact on the prosperity of the State was incalculable (Foley 1982, 28).

The original public corporation structure had been established in Victoria as a means of distancing government business enterprises from direct ministerial control and achieving greater public sector efficiency. However by the early 1980s this lack of direct accountability was perceived to be a major obstacle to ministerial responsibility and public accountability for government activity in the Victorian public sector. In an attempt to give cabinet more control over its public policy formulation, the Hamer Liberal government established a 38 member State Co-ordination Council composed of representatives of the biggest statutory corporations and departmental heads. However this unwieldy body proved ineffective in bringing the corporations to heel, and the problem of co-ordinating public policy in Victoria remained unsolved.

Exasperated by the corporations' intransigence that seemed to be a product of their independence, Hamer then set up a Public Bodies Review Committee (chaired by Dr K Foley) to explore the ramifications of corporation autonomy in the government's public sector agencies. The committee identified more than 9,000 operative public bodies, and went on to argue that their sheer number and variety, and their distance from the budgetary process made "the efficient management of the Victorian public sector virtually impossible". (Victoria, 1981 Public Bodies Review Committee)

The Committee's reports were presented to Parliament in 1981, and were to herald the end of almost a century of Victorian administrative history. The very feature deemed to be the statutory corporation's greatest virtue as an interventionist strategy in the early 1900s in Victoria, its independence from direct ministerial control, was now held to be its worst vice.

The Victorian branch of the Australian Labor Party(ALP), its long-standing left-wing and socialistic image softened by federal intervention and reconstruction in 1971, was quick to capitalise on public discontent with the State's creaking administrative system. They embarked on a major crusade for administrative reform in the structures of State government in the late 1970s and early 1980s, garnering much ammunition from the Liberal Foley Committee reports. These had exposed the inability of cabinet to set policy priorities due to serious deficiencies in the policy-making machinery, the division of responsibility for the allocation of resources between the Treasury and the Public Service Board, the organisational fragmentation of the public sector and the lack of an effective financial review process. It was all grist to Victorian Labor's campaign to win office and make democratic socialism an ideological reality in Victoria.

Its level of parliamentary representation bolstered by the 1979 State election, Victorian Labor set up a Working Party at the 1980 State Conference, for the express purpose of examining:

> [T]he organisational structure and administration of the Departments and Statutory Authorities that will be expected to implement the policies of a State Labor Government . . . [with the aim of recommending the] changes that will have to be made to achieve effective and equitable social, economic and physical planning for the people . . .
>
> Hudson 1983, 48

This Working Party's final report was to become the blueprint for direct government intervention in the Victorian economy by an elected State Labor government. In the 1980s the slogan became "socialism avec doctrines" and the State's well-being was entrusted to political leaders committed to administrative reform and the goal of implementing the principles of democratic socialism in Victorian government.

Victoria has a long history of ideological controversy and fervour, and Victorian Labor has also been the most ideological of all the ALP State branches, rarely winning State elections as a consequence. Political discussion and party debate, anchored in ideological difference is the key to Victorian State politics. Early in the 20th century radical political sentiment surfaced first in the agrarian causes espoused by the various country parties; if anything, Labor in Victoria lagged behind the other political parties in the pursuit of reform in Victorian government until the 1970s.[2]

After much debate and discussion in the late sixties, Victorian Labor Party idealists came to the conclusion that the problem was one of *implementing* the Party's democratic socialist ideology rather than reworking its principles; this they decided meant accepting the conventions of responsible government and working within the constrictions of the machinery of cabinet government to achieve their objectives. Their ideological thrust towards democratic socialism was retained, but the focus was now on the means whereby it could be implemented in the State of Victoria.

Thus when the first Victorian Labor government for almost 30 years took office in 1982, cabinet turned first to putting in place the reformed administrative structure it saw as critical to its goal of implementing the social, economic and physical policies it had spelled out in the election campaign. The historic Victorian pattern of an inner ring of Westminster model policy departments surrounded by an outer ring of strong autonomous corporations was abolished, and in its place the Cain cabinet set up for each area of government administrative machinery that it described as strong corporate management structures under firm ministerial direction. Responsibility for policy formulation and direction, overall control and accountability for each area was vested with the ministry, and the operating functions were hived off to agencies stripped of the autonomy that had been vested in the old public corporations.

In effect Cain Labor opted for a return to direct ministerial control as its preferred administrative strategy for ensuring that the Party's policy priorities would prevail. It was a return to 19th century Westminster conventions, leavened by the ideology of democratic socialism and modernised by late 20th century business administration principles as the means of ensuring efficiency in government, in place of the now discredited statutory corporations. Public sector utilities such as those providing electricity and water were stripped of their power to set their own priorities, and were directed to meet targets set by cabinet, instructed to operate on modern business lines, and required to contribute a 5% social dividend to consolidated revenue for community welfare, that is, they were now politically and socially directly accountable to their minister.

---

2 A discussion of ideology in Victorian politics, together with an account of the role of the Labor Party in Victoria is to be found in Parkin A and Warhurst J (eds), *Machine Politics in the Australian Labor Party*, Allen & Unwin, Sydney, 1983, Chap 3; also Holmes J, *The Government of Victoria*, UQP, 1976, Chap 6.

With this administrative machinery in place, the Cain cabinet pledged itself to bring unity, order and prosperity to the State of Victoria.

Paradoxically, this reformed administrative structure was to be a significant factor in the new State Labor government's eventual downfall. For cabinet government is party government (in Australia it is strong party government) and as FA Bland commented half a century ago in his book *Planning the Modern State*:

> [T]he excursions of government into business and trading are likely to be determined by *its own party interest* . . . suggesting the incompatibility of combining political and industrial functions . . . in a system of representative government.
>
> Bland 1945, 201-202 [author's emphasis]

The Cain Labor government's declared intention of exercising direct governmental control over its State enterprises paralleled the 19th century interventionist Victorian practices that had been abandoned when excessive political interference threatened government efficiency. Cain and his ministers were also to face political interference from the party factions and from the public sector unions in their second term in office, particularly in the areas of transport and education. Moreover the corporatist ethos on which the effectiveness of the new government's venture into State socialism had been founded had little in common with the party's democratic socialist principles, and eventually proved a source of serious conflict in the State's financial affairs.

Australia's colonial legacy of State intervention has given us an administrative history rich in examples of the basic instability inherent in organisations attempting to combine State enterprise and popular control. In the end Labor's innovative reforms to the machinery of Victorian government in the 1980s did little more than highlight the paradox that still confronts the modern interventionist democratic state. The fundamental contradiction between a Westminster parliamentary system and populist political culture is an unresolved problem still, and the following record of Victorian Labor in the 1980s only serves to highlight the conumdrum.[3]

3 For a full discussion of the issues touched on by this brief account see Weller P and Jaensch D (eds), *Responsible Government in Australia*, Australasian Political Studies Association, Richmond, 1980.

Labor's 1982 electoral victory

Euphoria gripped the Victorian branch of the Australian Labor Party in April 1982 when it was at last returned to office with a handsome election win. For 27 long years the government benches had been occupied continuously by the seemingly impregnable Victorian Liberal Party, and although the 1979 State election had seen Labor's Legislative Assembly seat total increase from 18 to 32, the Liberal and National Parties still held a respectable total of 49 seats between them in the 81-member house. In the early 1980s an ALP State electoral victory still seemed something of a mirage to many Victorian electors.

Several factors conspired to bring about the political sea change that gave Labor its landmark 1982 electoral victory. The Victorian electorate had become increasingly dissatisfied with the Hamer Liberal government's faltering economic performance and its apparent inability to manage the State's affairs. (Saulwick & Associates 1982) Victoria's Liberal premier, Sir Rupert Hamer, seemed little more than a shadow of his predecessor, the redoubtable Sir Henry Bolte, and his sudden resignation, leaving the Deputy Premier, Lindsay Thompson, to take over the party leadership shortly before an election date was announced added further to the electorate's disenchantment with the once powerful Victorian Liberal Party.

The Liberal electoral decline was paralleled by the transformation of the Victorian Labor Party branch in the latter half of the 1970s. Its historical left-wing and socialist image, a legacy of Victorian Socialist Party origins, had gradually become submerged in an aura of respectability, and by the early 1980s the party was perceived by the Victorian electorate for the first time for almost forty years as a credible alternative government. The party's new leader, John Cain, a conservative solicitor and son of the last Victorian Labor premier, epitomised Victorian Labor's “new look”. In the eyes of the electorate his “honest John', “squeaky clean” image confirmed the electoral suitability of the reformed Victorian branch of the Australian Labor Party for office.

The State Liberal Party's poor image was not helped by growing dissension within the ranks of the parliamentary party, compounded by a flare-up in the historical animosity between Victoria's two non-Labor political parties. (Costar 1985) The National Party even ran candidates in competition with the Liberals in selected country electorates, splitting the non-Labor vote in those areas and contributing its mite to an increasingly hostile country electoral environment for the Liberal Party. Nor was the city environment as friendly to the Liberals as it had been in the past. The emergence of a Labor-leaning minor party, the Australian Democrats as a significant force in State politics, and the simultaneous disappearance of the conservative Democratic Labor Party was symptomatic of the Liberals' declining electoral popularity in Victoria. The latter's second preference votes had helped keep the State Liberals in power since the ALP "split" in 1954-57 and its electoral demise was yet another blow to the State Liberal Party's political fortunes.

By 1982 this combination of the Hamer government's unpopularity with Victorian voters and the changing electoral environment was to rewrite Victoria's frozen electoral map. After 27 years in opposition the State electoral pendulum had finally swung the Victorian Labor Party's way. (Holmes 1984, Costar & Hughes 1983)

Cain Labor's blueprint for Victoria

The carefully thoughtout Working Party recommendations put before the State conference in 1981, together with a few additional conference resolutions constituted the State Labor Party's formal blueprint for Victoria's future economic prosperity. The new State government lost no time in spelling out its legislative program, stressing the primary role cabinet intended to play as in stimulating the lacklustre Victorian economy. Keynesian economic theory with its associated massive capital expenditures was the Cain cabinet's key strategy for achieving its self-proclaimed goal of restoring the State's economic vitality. (Victoria Government 1984a, Part A) The pump-priming policies put forward by the federal Chifley post-war Labor government had never been given a fair trial, said the new Premier; Labor lost to the Menzies-led Liberal/Country Party in 1949 and its visionary policies were never implemented. Now a State government intended to adopt those same policies and prove their worth in a depressed economy. (Cain 1985; Considine & Costar 1992, 5-7; Victoria 1984b).

While the Cain government stressed the initiative inherent in its plan to bring about a State-led economic recovery in Victoria, as noted earlier it was not the first time that a Victorian government had proposed the use of State intervention as a strategy for restoring the State's economic vitality. But Sir William Irvine's early 1900s corporations were independent enterprise agencies, set up at arms length from day-to-day politics and popular pressures. (Wettenhall 1985) By contrast, Cain Labor said unequivocally that it proposed to exercise "hands on" control over *all* aspects of the Victorian public sector to ensure that the government's policy goals were achieved. Victoria's new Labor government was to be corporate and management oriented, said the new premier; cabinet would function as a policy-oriented management team, working from the top-down, with direct accountability as the "bottom line". (Cain 1984)

From the outset the Cain Labor government insisted that a revitalised State government, innovative and vigorous, was the key to Victoria's future prosperity. Its cabinet was to be a circuit-breaker, a trail blazer for economic well-being and social justice, and they began their term in office by instituting far-reaching administrative reforms as their first priority.

> Unless you have the [reformed] structure, [said the Premier], you can't implement the sort of change we want to. A Labor Government has to be a government of change, and radical.
>
> *Age* 21 September 1983, 2

The Premiers' Department was reorganised so that it could be focused on policy and research rather than on the protocol of the past, and a rejuvenated Cabinet Office secretariat was set up to serve the cabinet and its active Cabinet committees, the heart of the new Labor administration. (O'Grady 1983, 206-23; 1985, 65-76) The old central public sector agencies were overhauled and the traditional Treasury Department replaced with a modern-sounding Department of Management and Budget under the direction of Dr Peter Sheehan, one of the architects of Victorian Labor's democratic socialism blueprint. (Sheehan 1980) His new department introduced far-reaching financial changes with program budgeting as a key strategy, and subjected the State's public service to major structural change to bring it into line with the modern business practices that were deemed critical to the government's plans. Westminster conventions of responsibility were phased out in favour of the catchword "let the managers manage" – managerialism became the new public sector religion in Victoria.[4]

"Getting the structures right" said the premier, was his government's first task if effective programs were to be put in place to achieve Labor's policy goals. It was cabinet's task to direct the State's economic resources to these goals, and the Victorian government was prepared and eager to take up "public sector equity in joint ventures with the private sector in areas where this will facilitate economic development". (Victoria 1984a, 3)

---

4 For a further discussion of Australian adaptations of the Westminster parliamentary model see *Current Affairs Bulletin* "The Westminster Model and Ministerial Responsibility" 61:1 June 1984.

All was grist to the Cain government's mill, with its fervent belief that a carefully thought out economic strategy for Victoria, under their firm control, would deliver the financial means and ample economic resources that would enable them to implement the Party's all important social justice goals.

Despite the centralist rhetoric of his government's policies and programs the premier insisted that his government's strategy should not be construed as a planning blueprint. The aim was to put in place a consultative program between the State's industries and the State government; Victoria's prosperity, he said, depended on co-operation between the public and private sector because:

> [T]he intention in Victoria is that the Government should facilitate and take an equity position in projects with strong growth prospects.
>
> Victoria 1984a, 3

With hindsight, it is doubtful if Victorian Labor perceived the possible consequences for a State government with an ideological conviction that Keynsian economic theory was an appropriate policy tool at the state government level.

In general economic pump-priming has tended to be a federal government function in Australia, and Cain Labor's financial inventiveness inevitably brought it into conflict with the federal Labor government. It can also be argued that in straying into areas somewhat removed from those central to traditional Victorian Labor Party ideology, it was inevitable that the government would be brought up short by its trade union member base and party factions intent on their own priorities. And finally, its social justice policies with their emphasis on State direction as the means of financing a comprehensive welfare state were to lead the State of Victoria into the overspending which precipitated a financial crisis from which the state is still recovering. The illusory ideology of government-generated resources in quantities sufficient to meet the Party's social justice goals for the state – improved health services and public housing, an education system geared to community demands, anti-poverty programs, urban redevelopment and so on – had by the end of its third term in office pushed Victoria's first Labor government in over a quarter of a century into a morass of collapsing financial institutions and corresponding community despair. A decade later, the vision of social justice funded by economic growth and efficient management has proved to be just that – a visionary dream.

The corporate state and creative accounting

The Cain government's rationalisation of its policies arose from its conviction that once a community has exchanged its votes for preferred policies at an election, day-to-day politics for a government with an electoral majority is a matter of optimising the social well-being of that choice. Policy choices become rational objectives for the party in power, political preferences conferring a mandate on an incoming government to give effect to the electorate's expressed wishes in its legislative, budget and tax policies. Such an obligation could only be successfully achieved if the government took a corporate approach, said the premier:

> Frankly I don't understand how anybody could hope to successfully run a government . . . without a corporate approach.
>
> Cain 1984

The prospectus for Cain Labor Incorporated was published as *Victoria – The Next Step: The Economic Strategy for Victoria*. Released in April 1984, it consisted of a series of detailed papers, almost 200 pages long, covering Labor's vision for Victoria. The government's: "expansionist macro-economic policies", it began, had contributed to the Victorian economy's rapid economic recovery from the 1982-83 recession, and it was now time to "address issues of economic strategy . . . [for] the development of the Victorian economy over the next decade". A prosperous, equitable and fulfilling life for all Victorians was the goal, pursued through the medium of the Economic Strategy to help redress social problems arising from unemployment, make the distribution of income more equitable, and provide resources whereby the government could fund an ever-increasing level of social and community welfare.

Cain Labor's prospectus also stated that the role of the State government in promoting economic development in Victoria had been underplayed in the past, and that a `more positive and systematic delineation' of that role was needed. To this end Labor put forward a range of policy initiatives intended to promote and stimulate private sector investment and employment. A key proposal was the combination of public sector equity with the private sector in joint venture projects targeted towards preferred strong growth areas that would assist in the development of commercial projects, particularly in Victoria's trade-exposed sector. As part of its commitment to this policy Labor was to increase its stake in the Portland aluminium smelter project established by the Hamer Liberal government, a decision that was to add substantially to the State's indebtedness. Wages and industrial relations policies, business costs, regulation and the efficiency of the public sector and the State's capital markets all came within the parameters of the Cain government's policy ambit, underpinned by its confidence in its ability to manage successfully the affairs of the State.

The sweeping nature of the Labor cabinet's corporate strategies for Victoria (Part B of *The Next Step*) makes awesome reading in today's straitened times. They saw the operation of the State's capital markets as critical to cabinet's planned economic growth, and the government's role in ensuring an efficient capital market as a vital one. The State-owned financial institutions, the Victorian Economic Development Corporation (VEDC), the Victorian Investment Corporation, the State Bank of Victoria, the Rural Finance Commission and the State Insurance Office, were all central to this strategy of government control of the State's capital market. The Cain government's confidence that its skills would enable it to manage Victoria's capital markets effectively is set out in the four objectives in its Economic Strategy statement:

> i. to ensure the efficient and effective management of its own funds
> ii. to provide funding to ensure that its policies in respect of the private sector will be implemented
> iii. to ensure the imperfections in the capital market are corrected
> iv. to provide support which will assist in the fulfilment of its social objectives
>
> Victoria 1984a, 64

As one commentator said, it was a "vision of a brave new world . . . where a Labor State Government would embrace and nurture private enterprise in a 10-year strategy to engineer economic security". (Bottom et al 1991, 171)

The confidence, and even passion, with which the Labor cabinet set about its mission to bring the State of Victoria into the "brave new world" of corporatism for the greater community good is evident in every page of its economic blueprint. It would not be necessary to provide more *public* resources, it said; it was just a matter of re-ordering priorities "within the existing volume of resources and the increased efficiency of their use". (Victoria 1984a, 183) Outmoded Westminster public accounting procedures were to give way to efficient management processes and the government's accountability to the people of Victoria would be demonstrated by the increased prosperity that would flow to them from that efficiency.

This firm determination to steer the "ship of state" in their chosen direction shaped the government's decision to return to centralised State development funding. To this end the old statutory corporations and public authorities were directed to transfer their substantial in-house sinking funds (euphemistically described by the Treasurer as "hollow logs") to the newly set-up Victorian Development Fund (VDF), an autonomous public financial authority with responsibility for allocating all funds for State development works and programs according to cabinet priorities. (Victoria 1983)

Centralised control places a heavy burden on the accuracy of the economic analysis tendered to governments if the State's development funds are to flow to areas where they are to be the most effective. In the new corporate Victoria the Economics Committee of Cabinet, consisting of the premier's senior ministers, was responsible for considering economic proposals and taking the appropriate economic decisions. Responsibility for the *implementation* of cabinet's Economic Strategy devolved onto the reconstructed Department of Management and Budget, headed by the Treasurer (Jolly). The Department's director, Dr Sheehan, set up a Policy and Planning Division to formulate public authority policy and economic policy, both short and long term, and to co-ordinate economic strategy and Commonwealth/State relations. So that the Department could achieve the government's missions and targets, budgeting and financial planning processes within the central agencies and departments were required to conform to Management and Budget's programs and capital budgeting processes. Its Policy and Planning Division also developed new financial systems to ensure better management of the government's asset portfolio.

Corporate planning processes, mission statements, quantifiable achievable objectives, upgraded information systems, and an increased capacity to review programs against government objectives were some of the new buzz words that replaced the very different language of State cabinet government in the past. The ethos of managerialism permeated the Cain government's new centralised structures of government, transforming Victoria's public sector in its heady first term. (Gregg, 1990) It would not have been possible, said Treasurer Jolly, to have implemented Labor's policy goals with the public sector administrative processes that the government had inherited; reforms to public sector management in Victoria were fundamental to the successful development of the State for the next decade. (Victoria 1984b)

The story of the Cain government's radical reform of Victoria's fragmented administrative structures is outside the scope of this chapter. However the subsequent financial consequences of replacing the traditional accountability patterns characteristic of Westminster systems with the vagaries of the corporate productivity ethos casts doubt on their usefulness in the Victorian public sector. (Painter, 1987, 133-152)

Ideology – the cruel experiment

Labor's emphasis in its initial term on administrative reform as the first stage of a new economic strategy found considerable favour with its new power base. ALP voters in Melbourne's middle class eastern suburbs now out-numbered the Party's western suburbs working-class supporters, and many of the new members of parliament swept into power in 1982 were professionals. They placed Victorian Labor's cherished social reform policies on hold for the first term to allow the new government to concentrate on its administrative reform program. However, when Labor was re-elected in March 1985 for a second parliamentary term (now four years in Victoria), the Cain government announced that the pragmatism of its first term was now to give way to the pursuit of the social goals integral to Labor's democratic socialism ideology. This new welfare thrust was spelled out in the Governor's speech at the opening of the new Parliament. Victoria was now leading the nation's economic recovery, it reported, and it was time to focus on the difficult social issues confronting the state and to address the question of social justice for all Victorians.

The 1985-86 budget reflected Labor's optimism about this change in political direction. It was time to restrain recurrent spending, slow down capital spending and balance the budget, said the Treasurer, time to initiate the government's social justice program. First targets would be the new worker's compensation program (Workcare) and improved health services, followed by increased funding for youth work/study programs, the anti-poverty program, public housing, and police and emergency services. Future capital expenditure would be targeted towards social areas (housing, health, corrections), and to joint ventures and initiatives in advanced technology. (Victoria 1985, 1; Victoria 1986a)

The broad objectives of the Cain government's social reform policies were later spelled out in its Social Justice Statement released in May 1986:

- to overcome unfairness caused by unequal access to economic resources and power . . .
- to guarantee equal legal, industrial and political rights . . .
- to ensure greater equality of access to essential goods and services, with particular attention to geographically related inequalities . . .

- to ensure expanded opportunities for genuine participation by all Victorians in the decisions governing their lives.

It is "a blueprint for a long-range, far-reaching reshape of social and economic resources, power, access, services, and rights, with the central aim of improving equity and fairness", said the premier: "We do intend to change things". (Victoria 1986b, 1)

Thus in its second term, the Cain government pinned its ideological colours to the wall. It was not enough for governments to spearhead economic growth and trust that everything else will fall into place, said the premier:

> Social policy must provide the steering mechanism for a reformist government . . . [although it] cannot meet the challenge alone . . . We will be looking to all sectors of Victorian society – welfare, business and industry, the unions – to be sensitive to social justice issues.
>
> (Victoria 1986b, 2)

Yet by 1992, despite highminded commitment to major social reform, Victoria's first Labor government for a quarter of a century was to be dismissed from office amidst mounting state debt and voter disenchantment. Some of the critical financial problems in its loans programs that were eventually to bring about Labor's downfall were already surfacing by mid-term. Its major loans corporation, the Victorian Economic Development Corporation (VEDC), set up to provide risk capital to the "strong growth" areas in the private sector, appeared to be in financial difficulties from early 1988 onwards, and rumours of its financial indebtedness appeared to trigger the premier into calling an early election in October 1988. Labor scraped back into office, but post-election press revelations of the VEDC's uncertain financial position left Cain's cabinet little option but to set up an inquiry into the operations of the VEDC. Tabled in the house on 21 December 1988, the Ryan report found that the VEDC was virtually insolvent, with losses of around $111 million resulting from the collapse of many of the companies to which it had made loans under the government's direction. (Bottom et al 1991, 175)

The sale of the State Bank of Victoria early in 1991 to the Commonwealth Bank of Australia was the outcome of similar financial misfortune. Its commercial subsidiary, the merchant bank Tricontinental had accumulated debts amounting to over $2.7 billion, threatening to bankrupt the State, and the new premier, (Joan Kirner) was forced to sell the parent state bank for a sum that was still insufficient to meet the subsidiary Tricontinental's debts. The costs of the State Bank's venture into merchant banking are now being written off by Victorian taxpayers, and the State is still recovering from the outcome of the innovative financial strategies that marked the Cain Labor government's venture into Victoria's capital markets.

The much-heralded introduction of program budgeting to the State financial accounts also appeared to do little to help the government achieve its widely publicised objectives. It was intended to aid cabinet policy choices and set out firm government directives for the Victorian business community, thus linking Victoria's prosperity directly to the economic analysis available to the government. In effect it was a strategy set up to give substance to the budget policies necessary to implement the government's desired social program. The then Treasurer (Jolly), spelt out this explicit link between Labor budgetary policy and social policy when he introduced his 1983-84 budget:

> A Budget is more than a financial statement – it is a social, economic and political document . . . the financial expression of the ideas and desires for the future direction of a government.
>
> Victoria 1984c, 3

By August 1990 the deterioration in the State's finances was all too apparent, and John Cain decided to resign as premier, his popularity at an all time low of 18 percent. He was replaced by the socialist left's candidate, Joan Kirner, who became Victoria's first woman premier. However, she too failed to restore Victoria's finances in the short time left to her, and the Party was unable to win back sufficient voter confidence before the October 1992 election. Electoral retribution was to catch up with the party and Labor with 38 percent of the primary vote, was reduced to 27 seats in the 81 member Legislative Assembly, and 5 seats in the Legislative Council.

For Victorian voters in October 1992, the price they paid for Labor's attempt to implement democratic socialism at the state level appeared to be a high one. The Cain/Kirner Labor governments had spelled out the ideological basis for their policies in their 1986 Social Justice Statement, but the rhetoric had a hollow ring for voters when the level of debt incurred by Victorian Labor in pursuit of its goals was revealed by the Nicholls Report in 1992. A previous party secretary pointed to the mitigating substance of social change brought about by the Cain government, encompassing a four or five inch thick computer printout. The difficulty with this justification is that few of the changes are likely to survive the Kennett Liberal government's cutbacks. Perhaps, as one more sympathetic account of the Victorian Labor years comments, the "Cain and Kirner [Victorian Labor] governments deserve a better epitaph than the one left them by the financial crisis and factional decay of their last years". (Considine & Costar 1992, 9) In the end their record will be judged by history.

Hidden agendas, economic mismanagement and accountability

How did a government so convinced of the merit of its economic and financial reforms, and of the moral worth of its program for social change fall into such disarray? Was it, as some have argued, because Labor in government is destined to self-destruct, so flawed that in office it inevitably cracks? Or was the problem the old one of Labor parties in office becoming captives to their trade union support base, which in turn constrains their options for independent decision-making?

One of premier John Cain's ex-advisers (Richards) has argued that temperamentally, the Labor Party is "strong on soul but weak on requirements for the long haul in government", lacking the necessary qualities for office of discipline, moderation and pragmatism. (Richards 1992, 15) Victorian Labor came to office, he said, with obligations to public sector unions whose 19th century approaches to work practices seriously constrained the Labor government's options for managing key public services. Richards went on to comment that fundamental management reforms in the health, education and transport services were kept off the Cain/Kirner government's political agenda as a consequence of its commitment to the public sector unions.

As he saw it also, the Cain government's lack of business experience (there were only two ministers in the first Cain cabinet with any business experience at all), and their scepticism about the established business elites was another problem. This suspicious stance meant that Labor governments either forged alliances with "high fliers" (a similar criticism was made of the Burke government in Western Australia), or maintained a disdainful distance from key business sectors with their knowledge of sound business management of deficits, debts and the commercial marketplace, business experience that might well have prevented some of the worst financial excesses. Labor's networks, said Richards, are party, faction and union, but almost never business.

The ex-premier, John Cain, also pointed to the strengths and weakness of left, right and centre factions in the Labor Party and to its links with unions as an important cause of the party's failures. (Cain 1992a, 11;

1992b 11; Cain 1992c, 280) He considered that the factions, with their formal memberships, constitutions, rules and fee structures had made an important contribution to the Victorian Party's 1982 electoral victory. By the latter part of the 1980s, however, he came to the conclusion that their influence was clearly alien to Westminster conventions of responsibility. According to the former premier, direct non-parliamentary factional involvement in pre-caucus meetings had become the accepted practice by the end of the government's second term. Factional balance determined the composition of the cabinet and its cabinet committees by 1988, giving the political executive a dominant left cast. Ministerial advisers were often factional watchdogs, and jobs were spread around the principal factions:

> [M]inisters and the factions driving them were determined to get their people into jobs across a range of areas to ensure them direct influence on decisions of government, [he said].
>
> Cain 1992a, 11

Thus, the former premier said, cabinet decisions came to be based not upon what was correct, but "simply on what was perceived to be in the faction's interest". Factional leaders appeared to know what was on the cabinet agenda, and if it included sensitive issues like Workcare, ministers always received "Sunday evening phone calls". Pressure was put on ministers to contract work away from one firm to another, said Cain, going on to describe how the trade union head John Halfpenny sought to overturn the government tendering process in favour of a firm whose tender price was $7 million rather than successful tender price of $3.5 million, and so on. Cain's examples pinpoint issues involving the transport unions, health care unions, and Work Care as key factional concerns, and he concludes by saying that the political fall-out was devastating:

> [T]he Government was seen as not being the master of its own destiny, and being the puppet on the end of strings pulled by the party factional bosses.
>
> Cain 1992a, 11

No clearer proof of the validity of Bland's 1945 proposition that party interest will always override proper business decisions by a representative government could be found. (see p 6)

More sympathetic observers (Considine & Costar 1992, 1) considered that Victorian Labor's collapse could be ascribed partly to a loss of impetus when the broad reform movement that had swept it into power gradually withered away. Moreover they said, State-based interventionist policies will always founder if the federal government pursues "a diametrically opposite program".[5] In their view it was doubtful if any State government could have survived the Victorian financial crises of the late 1980s; much of the criticism levelled at the Victorian Labor government for its financial mismanagement of the State's public sector should be directed at its appointed managers in whom they "put inordinate faith", but on whom they were unable to pin the blame for their failures when the crunch came.

Yet this is the crux of the Cain/Kirner Labor governments' public record. Westminster conventions of government place responsibility for the management of the public sector squarely on cabinet and the ministers of the Crown. Moreover Victorian Labor always placed considerable stress on the fact that *cabinet* policy choices dominated the policy process, particularly in its first term. Its first priority in government was to create a reformed bureaucracy under its firm political direction and control, insisting that the public service must be fully responsible to cabinet. In denying that Victoria's two Labor governments were responsible for the behaviour of their own agencies, Considine and Costar were also denying the canons of accountability central to the principles of a Westminster-based parliamentary democracy.

Economic mismanagement

A less sympathetic observer described Victoria at the end of Labor's third term in office as an:

> [A]ppalling mess, the product of bad government, massive property speculation, financial scandals, a tariff-dependent industry sector, national recession and a bloody-minded union movement deeply entrenched in the public sector.
>
> Wood 1992, 20

By the middle of 1991 criticism of Labor's State interventionist policies had begun to surface amidst fears that the State of Victoria was on the brink of bankruptcy and the premier Joan Kirner commissioned an independent audit committee to report on the State's finances. The committee, chaired by Don Nicholls, a public finance analyst with the stockbroking firm of McIntosh Securities, presented its report towards the

5 However, the Cain government planned to pursue interventionist policies at the State level from the outset, irrespective of any federal limitations that might limit their applicability at the State level.

end of September. Its findings were unequivocal – Victoria's budgetary position was unsustainable, it said, with:

> [A] significant and growing debt problem, particularly within the budget sector of Government where revenues have not been sufficient to the cover the Government's *operating* expenses for the last three years . . . unless the Government takes firm action . . . its indebtedness will continue to outpace revenue growth.
>
> Nicholls 1992, 19 [author's emphasis]

The Nicholls report went on to single out some of the key factors responsible for the State's present financial crisis. These included the government's strategy of financing budget-sector expenditure by short-term borrowing, the "black hole" of Public Transport Corporation losses, the level of non-debt liabilities including superannuation, Workcare liabilities, the provision of a flexible tariff electricity supply to the Portland aluminium smelters, and the financial deficits arising from the activities of the Victorian Economic Development Corporation, the commercial arm of the State Bank of Victoria (Tricontinental), and the Pyramid Building Society.

In Nicholls view, the Cain/Kirner government's budgetary weaknesses had clearly contributed significantly to the excessive financial debts in Victoria's public sector. Despite rising interest rates Labor had been unwilling to abandon its strategy of borrowing against State revenue flows to finance on-going public sector expenditure, and it also failed to rein in successive annual budget deficits despite clear warning signals from the financial sector. Servicing this debt, Nicholls argued, will take at least 25% of the State's revenues for the forseeable future.

Other critics had a different explanation for the tragedy of the Cain government; the pity said one observer,"was that a government that began so well, had so many ideas and such an able, decent leader should have ended in such ignominy". (Colebatch 1992, 13)

Key economic management and social policies were determined by a small group of "like-minded crusaders', said Colebatch, their commitment bolstered by the optimistic financial support of the Department of Management and Budget headed by Dr Peter Sheehan, one of the architects of the Working Party's blueprint. He described it as a policy process precluding serious consideration of other policy alternatives; but again a tightly controlled centralised policy structure staffed by loyal followers had been the deliberate choice of the Labor government from the outset. If overly centralised control was a factor in Labor's downfall, it can be argued that Victoria's first Labor government in over a quarter of a century came to office carrying with it the seeds of its eventual downfall. If the tough fiscal policies and labour market reforms, particularly in public transport, education and health that the Liberal Kennett government has introduced are the consequences of the failure of the centralised machinery of government set up by the Cain cabinet, it is a sharp criticism of the sweeping administrative reform in which Labor placed its trust.

The Tricontinental debacle

Victoria's State Bank had been linked to a merchant bank since 1975, but it was not until 1985 that formal governmental approval was given for the purchase of Tricontinental. (Armstrong 1992, 46) This gave it the enormous commercial advantage of having a government guarantee, but there is no evidence that the premier or the Treasurer understood the financial ramifications of their decision to approve of the purchase of Tricontinental by the State Bank of Victoria. Nor did they appear to grasp the commercial significance of the high risk/high profit corporate lending policies pursued by the Tricontinental board. (Armstrong 1992, 47,49)

Ian Johns, the 32-year-old managing director appointed a year later, typified the "new look" entrepreneur that appealed to Cain Labor. Born in Queensland and lacking tertiary qualifications, Johns was not the norm in Melbourne banking circles, but the record Bank profits he generated were considered by the Bank board to be sufficient qualifications for his meteoric rise. Although initially the Bank was enormously profitable under his leadership, many of the loans he authorised were to associates such as Christopher Skase, Abe Goldberg, Alan Bond, and George Herscu, all corporate "high-fliers" of the 1980s. The sharemarket crash in October 1987 was the beginning of the end, and by May 1989, Tricontinental's irrecoverable losses amounted to a staggering $2.5 billion plus.

Nevertheless Treasurer Rob Jolly continued to assure parliament that the State Bank of Victoria had made adequate provision for Tricontinental's losses, a mistaken perception appearing to arise from the Labor government's faulty understanding of the status of a merchant bank in the banking system. Both the premier and the Treasurer apparently believed that the Reserve Bank was monitoring Tricontinental's financial position, whereas a Reserve Bank spokesman told the Royal Commission inquiry in 1990 that its practice was to accept the State Bank of Victoria's assurance that all was well with Tricontinental. By March 1990 Jolly tendered his resignation as Treasurer "because of the pressures" and the premier's dwindling party support saw him also resign five months later. The new premier, Joan Kirner, said that she had no option but to sell the State Bank to the Commonwealth Bank of Australia to offset as much of the Tricontinental loss as possible, and even after the sale the Victorian government was left holding approximately $700 million of Tricontinental's outstanding debts.

In August 1990, the Attorney-General (Jim Kennan) announced the appointment of a Royal Commission, chaired by Sir Edward Woodward assisted by Mr D Williamson, to inquire into the Tricontinental debacle. The government promised a thorough analysis of the disaster, but the Commission did not submit its final report until two years later, just before the 1992 election on 7 September. The premier derived what political benefit she could from the Commission's report which exonerated the Labor government and said that it was not to blame for Tricontinental's financial losses.

The Attorney-General had also promised that the Commission would be a "most powerful inquiry" into the 1980s corporate failures, but this promise also proved somewhat illusory. The Commission had no sooner started its hearings when it found that the federal *Australian Securities Commission Act*, which came into force early in 1991, limited its ability to force witnesses to answer possibly incriminating questions at a public hearing. Ian Johns, Tricontinental's entrepreneurial managing director, was able to exploit this legality to his full advantage. He gave only very general evidence at the hearing before refusing to answer further questions about loan details on the ground that his answers might incriminate him, and the Victorian Supreme Court subsequently upheld his right to refuse to answer questions relating to his role as managing director which he did not wish to answer.

The report went on to say that nevertheless the Commission had not been "seriously inhibited in its inquiries by Johns's unwillingness to cooperate". It spelt out the magnitude of the Tricontinental debacle – losses equal to 37 times profits earned and nearly two-thirds of its total loan portfolio, losses which were 24 times its entire capital base and more than twice that of the State Bank of Victoria. All due to, said the report:

- placing too much emphasis on chasing market share as it sought to become Australia's largest merchant bank.
- the policy of high risks for high fees taken too far.
- an unacceptable concentration of risk with large loans to a few high-risk clients.
- over emphasis on lending for share purchases and property development.
- too little emphasis on sources of servicing and repayment of loans.

- the poor quality security for loans which were likely to dissipate if called upon.
- an approval process which sacrificed quality for speed with no proper evaluation of risks

(*Age* 1992a)

In the Commission's view responsibility for these "mistakes" rested clearly with the managing director, Ian Johns. It reported that he kept the bank's activities under his personal control, failed to share responsibility with the board of directors, and countenanced no checks and balances to his decisions. His serious personal failings –arrogant over-confidence, lack of business acumen, naivety in his dealings with his clients, and unwillingness to admit to his mistakes, together with his gambler's instincts– were such according to the Commission, that the collapse of the Tricontinental house of cards was inevitable. Johns, said the Commission "elected to perform his task at Tricontinental as if the bank was his personal property . . . his poor judgement and exaggerated idea of his own abilities was at the heart of Tricontinental's failure".[6]

However the Commission expressly rejected the notion that Johns's conduct was aimed at his personal gain, accepting that the decisions that brought about Tricontinental's huge losses were made by him "in the belief that they were in the best interests of the group". His were the faults of an over-confident gambler, not of a criminal, nor were any of the other managers guilty of personal misconduct according to the Royal Commission. They had committed errors of judgment, and even of negligence, but always they believed that they were doing what was expected of them by their managing director and the board of directors.

The Commission did find that the board of directors had a corporate responsibility for the collapse of the bank. It had approved of the high-risk lending strategy with its inadequate guidelines, and their report said its members, too complacent about their "one man band" chief executive, had ignored questions of accountability even if they were raised. The chairman of the board, Neil Smith, made it clear in his evidence that he had great faith in Johns, but, said the Commission it "was not able to place a great deal of confidence in Smith's evidence". His lack of attention to the details of Tricontinental's lending program together with his limited understanding of the intricacies of merchant banking came in for the commissioner's sharp criticism.

---

6 An analysis of some of John's transactions with his small group of entrepreneurial clients was published by Trevor Sykes in *The Bulletin*, 7 July 1992, 75-79. It was entitled "Tri, Tri Again".

The Commission was also critical of the failure of the Reserve Bank of Australia to carry out the watchdog role it considered it had accepted in 1986 when the governed-owned State Bank had entered into a voluntary agreement with the Reserve Bank to observe its prudential guidelines on the relationship between loans and capital resources. The Commission accepted that the Reserve Bank had no formal statutory authority over Tricontinental or its parent, but it had undertaken a monitoring role, and in that capacity it had apparently become concerned about Tricontinental's management as early as March 1988. However, in giving evidence before the Royal Commission the Reserve Bank spokesman made it clear that the Bank saw its voluntary responsibilities as applicable to the State Bank only, and it had simply accepted the latter's assurance that Tricontinental was under control.

Despite the weight of the evidence, the Commission did not consider that there was a case for recommending widespread criminal prosecutions, nor did it suggest that the Westminster conventions of collective and ministerial responsibility had any relevance.

> The important facts to emerge from this inquiry [they said], are that, disastrous as the Tricontinental losses have been, they did not stem from government failures, an incompetent bureaucracy, official or commercial corruption, or indeed any behaviour that could fairly be called criminal. They were essentially caused by ordinary human failings, such as the careless taking of risks while chasing high rewards [in a decade noted for its commercial greed], complacent belief in the reliability of others, lack of attention to detail, and arrogant self-confidence in decision making . . . all of which resulted in poor management and unsound business judgments.
>
> *The Age* (1992a)

The Commission went on to decide that it would not be easy to establish on the evidence available that any of their individual errors of judgment actually amounted to a breach of the *Companies Code* dealing with directors' duties. In seeking to prosecute the directors and managers all that would be achieved would be heavy legal costs on both sides and modest fines.

> The Commission strongly recommends against such action being taken.
>
> *The Age* (1992a)

Only three volumes of the four volume report were released in September. The last volume, dealing with potentially more serious charges, remained confidential because of the Commission's "deep suspicions" about the possibility of warehousing and insider trading in some of the share deals

Tricontinental undertook for its clients. It had been unable to reach firm conclusions, it said, but further investigation appeared to be warranted. Johns eventually was to serve a short prison sentence on the charge of accepting Commissions from clients, but no further prosecutions have eventuated.

It was estimated that Tricontinental's lending spree is likely to cost $630 for every man, woman and child in Victoria. One observer commented that the attitude and behaviour of both the State Bank and its "lunatic subsidiary" appeared to have been coloured by a belief that Victorian taxpayers stood behind them as a capital supplier of last resort. Sadly their assumption (whether conscious or otherwise) has become the State's reality today. (Bartholomeuz 1992, 13)

The failure of state corporatism in Victoria

Victorian Labor celebrated 10 years in power at a suitably subdued gathering held in March 1992 at the Moonee Ponds Town Hall, following the State Conference. With the government's initial enthusiasm and optimism a distant memory, few party members appeared to have the energy to think through what had gone so wrong for the Victorian Labor government swept triumphantly into office in 1982. Its front-bench, advocates of the visionary Social Justice blueprint, to be funded by the efficient management of the state of Victoria as a profitable corporation, now appeared to be fragmented, scattered and disillusioned.

Labor's vision for Victoria had also resulted in considerable upheaval in the Victorian public sector. It had been subjected to radical changes to its personnel and financial systems, and to a number of "reforms" to the accountability procedures used in its operating agencies; it had survived the development of "modern" organisational structures, and seen senior managers recruited from outside the public sector to staff the management "teams" of the new "responsive" public service system that Cain Labor considered essential. (Cullen 1986; Holmes 1987) In the end Labor's changes and reforms appear to have achieved little, and the concept of State corporatism seems as discredited as that of the autonomous Victorian statutory corporations of the past.

Quantifiable achievable objectives were to be the measure of Labor's efficiency in government, and judged by these criteria, Cain/Kirner Labor failed to achieve the economic goals set out in its corporate prospectus, *Victoria – the Next Step*. Labor's determination to take an aggressive role in promoting economic development in Victoria as the first step towards achieving its broad social goals resulted in two of its key financial institutions, the Victorian Economic Development Corporation, and the merchant arm of the State Bank of Victoria (Tricontinental), becoming virtually bankrupt. Its commitment to macro-economic strategies to promote economic recovery in Victoria had left the State with an unemployment rate of almost 12% in 1993, and according to the 1992 Nicholls inquiry, with an "unsustainable budgetary position" and a "significant and growing debt problem". If Victoria Incorporated was to be judged on its record, it would be included among the commercial corporate failures of the turbulent 1980s.

With John Cain's resignation in 1991, the new premier, Joan Kirner, turned her attention to tackling Victoria's financial problems. She began by stating that she was committed to taking the "hard" budget decisions necessary to reduce the state's indebtedness, and released an economic statement setting out a three-year debt reduction plan, estimated to reduce the 1991-2 budget deficit to approximately $839 million. However cabinet, faced by factional pressure to bring down an expansionary recession budget, failed to support the Premier's debt reduction target and it quietly disappeared.

Premier Kirner also included in her economic statement a proposal to corporatise the State's dependent statutory authorities into separate commercial entities subject to broad government direction only, that is, they were to be given an independent status characteristic of the familiar public corporations set up by the Liberal Irvine government in the early years of the century. This proposal to return to the traditional public authority structure also met with strong opposition from the public sector unions, and the subsequent bitter cabinet debate about its merits saw the premier abandon her attempts to reform the public sector altogether. With this reversal of political will by the Kirner Labor government in April 1992, Victoria's longest serving Labor government went into election mode by the middle of 1992.

To what extent the failure of accountability of the Cain government's corporatist structures which had replaced the previous Westminster derived public sector machinery of government had contributed to the Labor Party's 1992 electoral defeat is a moot point. John Cain believed that the emerging factionalism in Labor's third term in office which reduced the government to "being a puppet on the end of strings pulled by the party factional bosses" was critical to the party's downfall. Others argued that a public sector based on the corporate ethos should have been impervious to the kind of direct political pressure from the party factions described by the ex-premier, and that the ineptness of many of the private sector managers brought in to run public service institutions was the problem. The former Treasurer (Sheehan) claimed that the State Treasury was less than efficient, and had failed to give him accurate revenue figures or a true picture of Victoria's debt problems. Other critics in turn argued that the government had kept too tight a rein on the line departments and had been too lax with many of its agencies in a random application of corporate "bottom line" accountability which allowed excesses to go unchecked. (Cain 1992a, 11; Cain 1992b, 11; Merrigan & Forbes 1992, 6; Ellingsen 1992, 11) Undoubtedly all of these factors contributed to the final collapse and, taken together, they highlight the ineffectiveness of a Westminister based system in a environment hostile to its basic canons of responsibility.

For while the Royal Commission's findings exonerated the government from any responsibility for Tricontinental's failure, the report was highly critical of the lack of accountability procedures uncovered by its inquiry. It seems reasonable to assume that the Tricontinental example was indicative of the Cain/Kirner government's general failure to set up effective machinery to enable it to scrutinise the activities of its own agencies. The economic mismanagement that led to its financial downfall appears to have been as much a consequence of this absence of conventional public service accountability as anything else. In equating the corporate concept of accountability, with its focus on "bottom line" outcomes, to the Westminster conventions of responsibility that have shaped Australian parliamentary democracy, Victoria's Labor government lost financial control of its own agencies and ultimately, it also lost its own financial credibility.

The post-election revelation that the Kirner government had been funding recurrent expenditure with 90 day bills was yet another shock to the Victorian community, and the subsequent disclosure that its borrowings had exceeded Victoria's Loan Council limits by $1.5 billion added to public concern. (Ellingsen 1992, 11) Victorians are now living with the fall-out from the Cain/Kirner governments' failure to manage their State's business affairs with sufficient efficiency and propriety and the discredited State authorities are in the process of being dismembered and privatised by the Kennett Liberal government which was subsequently voted into office by a disillusioned state electorate.

The 1992 election campaign and the "politics of blame"

In the run-up to the 1992 State election day (3 October) Labor's new Treasurer (Peter Sheehan) diligently sought to find ways to improve Victoria's budgetary position, short of increasing taxes or cutting government spending, both strategies unacceptable to the factions and unions that constitute Victorian Labor's heartland. One of the more ingenious proposals canvassed by the new Treasurer was that of a complicated debt-for-equity swap whereby the government would take over responsibility for the long-term debts of the three major statutory authorities, (State Electricity Commission of Victoria, Victorian Gas & Fuel Corporation, and Melbourne Water), leaving them with their short-term debt only. The three authorities were to be restructured as commercial entities, still State owned, but with the existing board members being replaced by independent commercially experienced board members, charged with the specific task of improving agency efficiency. The increased interest costs to the government resulting from the acquisition of the old authorities' long-term debt was to be met from the projected higher social dividend payments that would flow from the increased productivity that could be expected of the new independent agencies. Incorporated as separate commercial entities they would take over the previous corporation short-term debt, gradually replacing it with new loans as the old ones matured. The effect would be to move about $5 billion of public debt progressively out of the public sector into the private sector, reducing the Victorian State's estimated indebtedness accordingly. In the end this scheme too, like so many others, fell foul of the strong public sector unions and cabinet abandoned it.

To counter the decline in State revenues (due to falling pay-roll tax and stamp duty collections and reduced federal government payments) and give some leeway for election promises, the Kirner government decided to beef up asset sales in the pre-election lull. These included the part sale of the partially completed Loy Yang B power station complex, and the transfer of the government's responsibility for the Portland Aluminium smelter subsidy (an estimated $217 million) to the State Electricity Commission of Victoria. The government even broached the possibility of requiring the statutory authorities to buy out the holders of $710 million maturing Victorian Equity Trust Bonds, arguing that the loans were nominally raised on their behalf. However, none of these desperate measures made much impact on the gloomy electoral climate, and the premier finally announced on 1 August that a poll would be held some time in October. The campaign proper had begun.

It appeared that the Kirner government's main election campaign problem was going to be its apparent lack of economic credibility, compounded by its failure to make progress with the debt management targets set out in its 1991 June economic statement. Faltering asset sales and a budget deficit likely to be double the targeted figure had played havoc with the three-year plan and its strict financial projections. In its stead the premier brought down an expansionary budget in September 1992, almost immediately afterwards announcing an October 3 election date. In effect the government had formally abandoned the financial goals it had set out a scant 14 months earlier.

Labor justified the decision to abandon the promised financial reforms by arguing that Australia's continuing recession, and the growing number of unemployed Victorians made an expansionary budget more appropriate. Cuts in the federal government payments to the States had contributed to Victoria's budget shortfall, and federal tariff cuts were blamed for Victoria's climbing unemployment. An election campaign strategy founded on the "politics of blame" saw the Labor Party sidestep criticism of its economic mismanagement and of the part it had played in the failure of the State's financial institutions. Instead it concentrated on raising voter anxiety about the likely impact of coalition policies on public sector services – on the loss of jobs and the corresponding decline in the State's essential public services that would follow. Victorian voters had the choice, said the Labor Party, between a caring and compassionate government that put people first, and an ideology-driven economic rationalist government of the kind that had failed so dramatically in New Zealand.

The Liberal and National parties campaigned in Victoria as a formal coalition for the first time in 1992. They too ran a "politics of blame" campaign, but they described Labor as "The Guilty Party". They pointed to Labor's spending spree in office which they said had bankrupted the State of Victoria and promised that a Liberal/National Party government would introduce far-reaching reforms and restore the State's economy to health again. Their plans included the reform of industrial relations and the Workcare scheme, and the transfer of a wide range of State services such as health, transport and energy to the private sector. They pledged the community that they would reduce the State debt by $8 billion by the turn of the century. A bigger revenue base arising from a revitalised private sector, said the Liberal/National Parties, was the key to restoring the

State's finances, and the only way to avoid the draconian rises in State taxes and public expenditure cuts that would otherwise be necessary. They did admit that some public sector work force reductions were inevitable, and also that further borrowings would be necessary to meet the cost of the redundancy payments involved. Pushed for details on the number of public sector jobs that would be lost under a coalition government, the opposition parties refused to spell out specific targets, an evasion that appeared to cause considerable concern to the big public sector unions that had benefited considerably under the Labor government.

Perhaps the final, and somewhat bizarre, comment on the 1992 Victorian election campaign was the emergence of a new political party, the Natural Law Party. It put forward a policy of transcendental meditation as the key to a revitalised Victoria.

> Victoria urgently needs a coherent, effective government. This can be achieved by 7000 [Victorians] meditating in a group to create a harmonious Victoria during the State election.
>
> (*Age* 1992b, 17)

Some thirty three independent candidates supported the meditation policy, and practitioners of transcendental meditation were invited by the party to attend group meditations on election day. The party's vote percentage was insignificant, but transcendental meditation parties have emerged in other western countries, including the United Kingdom. One common factor behind their appearance is a public distrust of government. In a long boring election campaign, during which the Victorian electorate's overriding need to "blame" and punish Labor for what it saw as its economic mismanagement rarely faltered, the emergence of a political party founded in distrust of government had a poetic symbolism.

A decade after its resounding election victory, the Victorian Labor government awoke on the morning after polling day in 1992 to an equally devastating defeat. The Victorian ALP primary vote percentage was down to 38%, and that of the coalition up to 52%, the latter now holding 61 seats in the 88-member lower house and a clear majority in the upper house. Labor in Melbourne has once again retreated across the Yarra River to its western suburbs stronghold, a heartland vote which gave the premier some consolation in defeat.

Five Labor ministers lost their seats in the massive swing to the coalition parties on 3 October, and the parliamentary superannuation entitlements were the largest ever paid out after a State election!

Victoria's future

Among the many post-mortems analysing Labor's defeat, a number pointed to the ideological difference between Labor and its opponents. Cain's senior adviser in the heady first term years was among them. Richards argued that the important philosophical divide between Labor and non-Labor was a key factor; non-Labor is concerned about wealth creation, he said, and Labor about wealth distribution, and Victoria's Cain/Kirner Labor government was true to type. (Richards 1992a, 15) This concern for a more equitable distribution of resources coloured all their economic planning said Richards, a conclusion illustrated by Cain's first Treasurer, Rob Jolly, when he said in *Victoria – The Next Step* (page 60) that Victoria's social infrastructure – citizen access to health, education, transport, recreation – was equally as important as the civil infrastructure of roads, railways, air and sea ports, energy generation facilities, sewerage services.

> The level of provision and maintenance of such infrastructure, [he said], is . . . the most obvious and available criterion upon which to measure the performance of Governments in a mixed economy.

Richards also argued that the Victorian Labor government concentrated on reforming the social infrastructure at the expense of financial management and public sector efficiency, the hard-edged aspects of government that are critical to establishing appropriate conditions for wealth creation and economic growth. Ironically, the Cain government, including the Treasurer was equally convinced that its financial and economic policies would restore Victoria's prosperity. Jolly concluded his Treasurer's statement on Victoria's opportunities for the 1980s by saying:

> The opportunities are there. The government can be relied upon to make Victoria more competitive and to support firms which grasp these opportunities. It is now up to the private sector to respond, to take the initiative and to confirm Victoria as a key growth centre of Australia.
>
> (Victoria 1984b, 36)[7]

Others have pointed to the problems that arose from the links between the Cain/Kirner governments' and the big public sector unions in transport,

7 Australia's Labor Prime Minister, Mr Keating, made a similar point in a recent television interview. Australia is locked into the fastest growing part of the world, he said, open to opportunities, with a low tariff wall, floating exchange rate, a free financial market, and better tax system. Australia in the 1990s is going to be in a very, very attractive position. "All we've got to do is get that recovery phase moving". For Victorians his words had a hollow ring. (ABC 1992)

education and health. The extent to which Labor was captive to the Trades Hall Council is difficult to assess, but both Labor Premiers have said that they were often frustrated by the unions in their efforts to introduce long overdue reform into the public sector workplace. (Cain 1992a, 11; 1992b, 11; Kirner 1992, 21) Cain said in 1992:

> The most potent external factors affecting government performance were the party factions and the way they undermined the government from early 1990.
> (Considine and Costar 1992, 280)

Richards said that in the mid-1980s the Labor Education Minister, Ian Cathie, had been a typical casualty of union power when he sought to modify the teachers' industrial agreement. The union was able to mobilise sufficient Party support to ensure he lost his portfolio and was dismissed. (Richards 1992b, 19)

The trade union leadership planned to flex its muscles as it confronted Victoria's new Liberal/National Party government, led by Premier Jeff Kennett. The latter moved quickly to introduce what it insisted were necessary economic, financial and industrial reforms, only to find that the Victorian community has been reluctant to part with the Labor Party's social benefits despite the costly public sector structure needed to service them. The full cost is still emerging, but the Auditor-General's 1992 report tabled in parliament at the end of October, some three weeks after the election, listed some of the financial outcomes of Labor's term in office.

Mr Baragwanath was appointed Auditor-General in 1988 after the previous Auditor-General (Humphry) had resigned to take an appointment in New South Wales. The new Auditor-General was often critical of the Cain/Kirner Labor government's financial strategies, and spoke out firmly when he felt that his proper access to official files was being impeded. (Baragwanath 1992, 1) His last report on the Kirner government's term revealed that it had understated its 1991-92 loan liabilities by $1.2 billion, deferred interest payments to improve its budget balance, entered into transactions outside budget parameters, and had made guarantees to private and public bodies without the knowledge of parliament. Westminster conventions clearly appeared to have been cast aside in the stress of the government's last few months in office. Government debts and liabilities now amounted to $41.3 billion, said the Auditor-General, with contingent liabilities of $22.6 billion. Among other items he said that the Kirner government had omitted to include in its budget papers were $422 million in transport leasebacks, $283 million in deferred payments, $158 million in delayed compensation for the Portland smelter unit trust, a $149 million debt on the World Congress Centre, $82 million in interest interchanges, and $66 million for the cost of privately-funded police stations and courts. Pointing to bids to improve its finances, he said that the government had sold the State Insurance Office for $214 million, failing to secure any return for goodwill, and it had also involved itself in potential liabilities of $140 million associated with the sale and redevelopment of the Queen Victoria Hospital site and St Vincent's Hospital. And so on.

The Auditor-General's report concluded by stressing that sound financial management based on debt reduction, the elimination of recurrent deficits and the reduced reliance on borrowings for the funding of government programs was critical to the long-term improvement in the State's financial position, and to the restoration of its international credit rating. According to the State's Auditor-General Victorian taxpayers will be paying for the failure of the State Bank, Tricontinental, the Pyramid Building Society, the Victorian Economic Development Corporation and the Victorian Investment Corporation well into the next century. (Vic (1992) *Auditor General's Report on Finance 1991-92*)

Conclusion

One of the sadder aspects of this report of Victoria's financial position is the sense of historical "deja vu" that it invokes. Describing the 1880s economic boom, Michael Cannon (1966, 3) wrote:

> Visitors to the colony of Victoria in the 1880s were awed and dazzled by the . . . capital city. They began to call it "Marvellous Melbourne". Everywhere they looked the humble buildings of the early colonists were being pulled down, and in their place were rising the great granite piles of a myriad financial institutions. In the suburbs . . . luxurious mansions were built by the score for the newly rich . . . Business boomed. Banking boomed. Money poured in from overseas. The frenzy grew and fed upon itself.

Inevitably, said Cannon, the 1880s "Victorian dream of eternal prosperity was converted into nightmare", and the failure of the State's democratic but immature political institutions to control the greedy speculators and banks in the 1880s resulted in the horrors of the 1890s depression. Many of the Victorian parliamentarians in the 1880s, he said, had little regard for their responsibilities to the community in their pursuit of private wealth, and even less understanding of the consequences of their unbridled greed. Yet despite the mountain of evidence of the consequences of unfettered private enterprise Cannon (38) noted that parliamentarians Murray-Smith and Grimwade were still affirming that "the permanent prosperity and progress of the State will be best secured by leaving to free and unchecked development the forces of individual energy and enterprise".

The parallel a century later is a poignant one. Victoria's Labor governments also appear to have been incapable of controlling the speculative behaviour and profligate spending of their own agencies. They appear to have been as incapable of reining in the public sector unions in the 1980s as the conservatives in the 1880s were in curbing the land speculators. Throughout the 1992 State election campaign, Premier Kirner defended Labor's policies of social justice for all, despite the "unsustainable financial situation" that those policies had created in the State of Victoria. Like Murray-Smith and Grimwade in the 1890s, Victorian Labor parliamentarians in the 1990s appeared to have persuaded themselves that the virtue of their cause outweighed the self-evident financial defects of its implementation.

The failure of the Westminster conventions of cabinet and ministerial responsibility and the associated machinery of government to check the financial excesses of the Cain/Kirner Labor government in the latter part of the 1980s raises serious questions about the nature of accountability in modern parliamentary democracies. The ethos of managerialism that dominated the Victorian public service under the Labor governments appears to have been a poor substitute for the traditional public sector procedures that it replaced, and the outcome of the managerialist ethos in Victoria raises considerable doubts as to its relevance in a public sector environment. The innovative corporatisation of the political and administrative structures of Victorian government that Premier Cain had so proudly introduced to pave the way for a democratic socialist state appear to have failed to deliver the policy objectives confidently set out in *Victoria – The Next Step.* If anything, its contribution was to worsen Victoria's Humpty Dumpty fall amidst an Australia-wide economic recession. Managerialism as a theory of administration offers little to a State faced with a long and painful economic recovery from its decade of Labor government.

References

The Age (1992a). Tricontinental Edition, 7 September.
—— (1992b). Natural Law Party Election Advertisement. *The Age*, 12 September.
Alford J (1992). Industrial Relations: Labor's Special but Difficult Relationship. In Considine M and Costar B (eds), *Trials in Power*, Melbourne University Press, 145-158.
Armstrong H (1922). The Tricontinental Affair in Considine M and Costar B (eds), *Trials in Power*, Melbourne University Press, 43-58.
Australian Broadcasting Commission (1992). *Lateline*, 19 November.
Bartholomeuz S (1992). The Buck Finally Stops in a Farce. *The Age*, 7 September.
Baragwanath C "Labor hid debt" in *The Age* 30.10.92 1.
Bland FA (1945). *Planning the Modern State*, Sydney, Angus & Robertson.
Bottom B et al (1991). *Inside Victoria*, Chippendale, Pan Macmillan.
Cain J (1984). *Public Administration and the Corporate Approach*, Address to Royal Institute of Public Administration – Victorian Division, February.
—— (1985). Address at University of Melbourne on 26 June, unprinted.
—— (1992a). Labor Factions at the Helm. *The Age*, 19 February.
—— (1992b). A Scratch that Became a Wound. *The Age*, 16 October.
—— (1992c). Achievements and Lessons for Reform Governments in Considine M and Costar B (eds), *Trials in Power*, Melbourne University Press, 265-280.
Cannon M (1966). *The Land Boomers*, Melbourne University Press.
Colebatch T (1992). The Getting of Wisdom and the Laying of Blame. *The Age*, 11 August.
Considine M and Costar B (eds) (1992). *Trials in Power*, Melbourne University Press, 1-10, 281-286.
Costar, B (1985) National-Liberal Party Relations in Victoria. In Hay, PR et al (eds) *Essays on Victorian Politics*. Warrnambool Institute Press. 157-165.
Costar B and Hughes C (eds) (1983). *Labor to Office – The Victorian State Election 1982*, Melbourne, Drummond.
Cullen RB (1986). The Victorian Senior Executive Service: A Performance Based Approach to the Management of Senior Managers, *AJPA*, XLV (1), March, 60-73.
Ellingsen P (1992). Labor's Loans Affair, *The Age*, 27 November.
Foley K (1982). Victoria's Quangos: the 1980s and Beyond in Davis SR et al, *Quangos: The Problem of Accountability*, Melbourne (Monash University, Centre of Policy Studies, Special Study 2, 28.
Gregg S (1990). Corporate Management in Australia: Reform or Reaction, *BA Honours Thesis*, Department of Political Science, University of Melbourne.
Holmes J (1976). *The Government of Victoria*, University of Queensland Press, Chap 6.
—— (1980). "State Government in Australia" in Understanding Public Administration, Special Issue of the *AJPA*, XXXIX 3:4 1980, 340-351.
—— (1984). Politics in Victoria – Ideology Regained. *Current Affairs Bulletin*, 61 (4), 18-31.
—— (1987). Administrative Chronicle for Victoria, *AJPA*, XLVI (2), June, 217-225.

Hudson G (1983). The Labor Party Campaign in Costar B and Hughes C (eds), *Labor to Office: the Victorian State Election 1982*, Melbourne, Drummond.
Kirner J (1992). ALP Lacked Resolve for Reforms, *Age*, 25 November.
Merrigan K and Forbes M (1992). A Decade of Dilemmas, *The Sunday Age*, 5 April.
Nicholls D (1992). Review of Victorian Public Finance, *The Age*, 22 September.
O'Grady M (1983). Labor and the Bureaucracy in Costar B and Hughes C (eds), *Labor to Office*, Drummond, Melbourne, Chap 16.
—— (1985). The Department of the Premier and Cabinet Under Labor in Hay PR et al (eds), *Essays on Victorian Politics*, Warranambool Institute Press, 65-76.
Painter M (1987). *Steering the Modern State – Changes in Central Coordination in Three Australian State Governments*, Sydney University Press.
Parkin A and Warhurst J (eds) (1983). *Machine Politics in the Australian Labor Party*, Sydney, Chap 3.
Richards M (1992a). Party of the '80s fatally flawed in key issues of government. *The Sunday Age*, 13 September.
—— (1992b). School of Hard Knocks. *The Sunday Age*, 22 November.
Saulwick & Associates (1982). Age Polls. *The Age*.
Sheehan P (1980). *Crisis in Abundance*, Penguin, Dominion Press, Blackburn, Victoria.
Spann RN et al (1973). *Public Administration in Australia*, Government Printer, New South Wales.
Steele Pamela (1983). The Media and the Cain Government in Costar B and Hughes CA (eds), *Labor to Office*, Drummond, Melbourne, 1983, Chap 14.
Victoria (1981). Public Bodies Review Committee (Chairman KJ Foley). *Report on a Study of the Audit and Reporting Responsibilities of Public Bodies in Victoria*, Victorian Government Printer.
—— (1983). *Victorian Notes*, 16.
—— (1984a). *Victoria – The Next Step*. 9 April, Part A, Melbourne, Government Printer.
—— (1984b). *Treasurer's Statement*, 9 April, Melbourne, Government Printer.
—— (1984c). *Program Budget 1983-84*, 1, Melbourne, Government Printer.
—— (1985). *Victorian Economic Report, 1*, Melbourne, Government Printer.
—— (1986a). *Partnerships in Technology for the 1990s*, Update, 10 August, Melbourne, Government Printer.
—— (1986b). *Update*, 7 May, Melbourne, Government Printer.
—— (1992a). Report of Auditor General on the Financial Statement 1991-2. Melbourne, Government Printer.
—— (1992). Report of Auditor General on Ministerial Portfolio's May 1992. Melbourne, Government Printer.
Weller P and Jaensch D (eds) (1980). *Responsible Government in Australia*, Australasian Political Studies Association, Richmond.
Wettenhall RL (1985). The Public Sector in Victoria: How Different? in Hay PR et al (eds), *Essays on Victorian Politics*, Warrnambool Institute Press, 27-48.
Wood A (1992). Taking Stock in Victoria, *The Weekend Australian*, 25-26 July.

2

South Australia:

Where Has All the Money Gone?

Ian Radbone

Introduction

By September 1993 the total amount needed to cover the losses of the State Bank was $3.15 billion. This figure represents the biggest single financial disaster to hit any government in Australia this century. If measured in terms of the size of the economy which has to bear the loss, the disaster dwarfs that of any other State. It represents over $2400 for every South Australian. And yet this is in a State which, the columnist PP McGuinness wrote in 1990, "has led an almost blameless existence for some years now as far as its fiscal affairs are concerned". (quoted, Parkin 1992, 18)

The explanations of financial disaster in Western Australia and Victoria involve many players and in the case of Victoria are at least partly due to the social and employment policies of the government. In South Australia, by contrast, we need look little further than the State Bank.

Almost single-handedly, the State Bank Group has wasted all the pain that went into reducing the State's public sector debt from 23.7% of gross State product in 1979-80 to 15.5% in 1989-90. Today debt stands at over 25%; the increase representing not investment in productive assets, but borrowings to cover losses.[1]

How was this disaster allowed to happen? Decisions made by managers in the public sector are subject to an impressive number of control and checking processes to prevent such a thing. Individual decisions are subject to control by the Bank's senior staff, aided by internal auditors. The actions of the senior staff are themselves overseen by the controlling body of the agency – in this case the State Bank's board. The

1 Figures are from South Australia, Treasury (1992) *table* 3.4. Note SAPD is South Australian Parliamentary Debates.

board's duties in this regard are informed by external auditors. The board itself is answerable to the responsible minister (the Treasurer) and through him, to parliament. The government's stewardship is assisted by the expertise of the Treasury. As well, although there were at the time no formal controls in place, in practice the government relied on the Reserve Bank's monitoring and checking influence. These checking and controlling relationships are illustrated in the following diagram.

Figure 2.1: State Bank: Accountability and information relationships

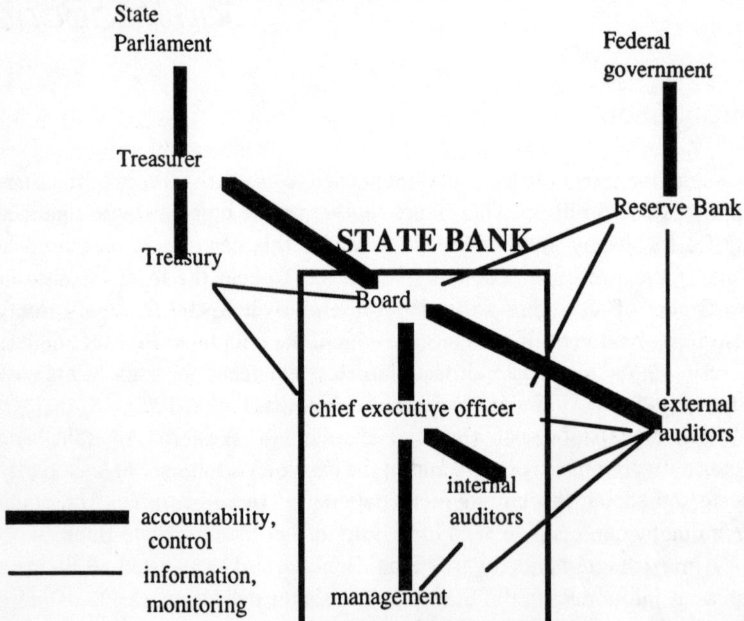

The first report of the Royal Commission into the State Bank of South Australia concluded with these words:

> The saga of the State Bank is . . . a story of inappropriate relationships and an unsatisfactory quality and level of communication between the Treasury and Treasurer; between the Treasurer and the Bank; between Treasury and the Bank; between the Board of the Bank, its Chief Executive Officer and its management; between the Reserve Bank and the Bank; and between the Reserve Bank and the Government.
>
> All these players played a part in the ultimate tragedy.
>
> Royal Commission, First Report, 392-393

This chapter will examine each of these links to examine why they failed. Before doing so, an account of events is in order.

A brief history

The State Bank was born out of a merger of the (old) State Bank of South Australia with Savings Bank of South Australia.[2] Both the constituent bodies dated from the 19th century. The Savings Bank of South Australia opened its doors in 1848 and although formally a government institution, it operated very much in the interests of the depositors. When the Kingston administration failed in its efforts to have the Savings Bank used as a channel for government loans for farmers and local government, it secured parliamentary approval for the establishment of the State Bank of South Australia. This commenced business in 1896. Its charter emphasised rural development and the encouragement of home ownership through low interest loans. It grew to be a key instrument in the implementation of State development strategies.

In 1983 the State government decided that the two banks should be combined to provide the necessary size to compete in the emerging deregulated environment. The bill merging the two banks was introduced into parliament in November 1983. The Treasurer's second reading speech noted that while operating within the "accepted principles of financial management", the bank should become "an active, innovative and effective participant in the South Australian economy and financial markets" (*SAPD*, 17 November 1983, 1935). The need for flexibility was mentioned several times.

The role of the merged bank in the economic development of the State was central, particularly given that the last private bank with its headquarters in South Australia (the Bank of Adelaide) had been swallowed by the ANZ a few years earlier. (*SAPD*, 6 December 1983, 2359)

The need for an aggressive, entrepreneurial strategy seemed to be underlined by the deregulation of the finance industry which was taking place at the same time. The relaxation of prudential controls and of controls over interest rates (particularly home lending), as well as the introduction of foreign competition by the federal government were all signals to the local banks that they had to become much more competitive in their service. The previously cosseted Australian banks were facing a

2 For a history of the banks, see Gobbett (1986).

new era in which – the conventional wisdom had it – those who did not compete aggressively for business would be swallowed by those who did. While the merged bank would be better able to face the competition from the large commercial banks, it would need to grow. As the slogan of the times had it: get big or get out.

Banks grew rapidly through the 1980s. The growth in the assets of the big banks averaged 17.7% a year during the period 1985-1990. But the State Bank grew even faster. Group assets (that is, total loans) expanded by an average of over 40% each year. Net assets grew apace.

Table 1: State Bank Growth

	total assets	**net assets**
30 June 1984	$3.1 billion	$173.7 million
30 June 1987	$7.9 billion	$592 million
30 June 1990	$21.1 billion	$1.38 billion

Royal Commission, First Report, 23

The bank also changed in nature. It was no longer primarily a South Australian operation. By 1990 two thirds of assets were interstate or overseas. Overseas assets grew from $200 million at the end of 1985 to $5270 million by February 1991. (Auditor-General, vol Xl, 23.13) It went from being a retail bank to one heavily involved in wholesaling funds for other financial institutions. Wholesale funds represented 15% of its business in 1984; 82% in 1990. (Auditor-General, 1993 vol l, 1.23) (referred to hereafter as Auditor-General).

Acquisitions were a prominent feature of the growth. Beneficial Finance was the first. Australia's 12th largest finance company in 1984, it grew under the State Bank umbrella to be fifth largest by 1989. (*Australian Financial Review,* 29 March 1989, 76) Helped by the threat of government legislation (*Australian Financial Review*, 27 December 1984, 24), the State Bank beat the ANZ in a bidding war for the old South Australian company, Executor Trustee, in early 1985. It bought half of the stockbroker, SVB Day Porter, at the same time. In 1986 it bought South Australia's largest real estate firm, Myles Pearce. In 1987 a merchant bank, Ayres Finniss, was established. In November 1988 it bought a small New Zealand bank, Security Pacific Bank New Zealand and Oceanic-Pacific Property Trust.

The conventional wisdom of the time was that banks had to develop an international focus. The big banks started opening offices overseas and acquiring foreign banks. Though the rationale for this was never really explained, let alone carefully analysed, the State Bank decided that it should follow this path too and opened branches in Hong Kong, London and New York. By the end of the decade the State Bank had 20% of its assets held overseas and was planning to double this proportion over the next few years. While the previous South Australian banks had had a presence in other States, these were essentially to serve South Australian clients doing business there. The new bank actively sought business outside South Australia, involving itself in undertakings with no apparent connection with the State.

But the biggest factor explaining the increased scale of operations was simply a far more aggressive lending policy. Furthermore, the focus of activities diverged dramatically from that of the progenitors. It still had an important role as a savings bank, but its trading activities moved well away from agriculture. Oddly, for a bank with a charter to promote economic development, the proportion of loans to agriculture, mining and manufacturing was smaller than that of the big private banks. After a corporate banking office opened in October 1985 the emphasis was on finance, investment and insurance as well as on property and business services. (Scott 1992, 91) It developed a reputation for providing the cheapest corporate finance in the country. (*Australian Business*, 10 June 1987, 105) All of these activities were lauded by the financial press. Rapid increases in the asset base were an indication that various State government-owned banks were "flourishing". (*Australian Financial Review*, 19 September 1986, 45[3]) This happy state of affairs continued even after the stock market crash of October 1987. In December 1988 both Moodys and Standard and Poors gave the bank their highest credit rating for its loan program to establish the New York office. (*Australian Financial Review,* 6 December 1988, 70) In 1988, accepting the State Bank's arguments that it was in a good position to expand, the State government invested a further $385 million in the bank. (*Triple A*, March 1989, pp. 16-19)

The first public doubts about the Bank were expressed in early 1989, following two financial disasters of the time, the collapse of Equiticorp and the National Safety Council. It was revealed that the Bank was one of the main creditors in each case. Exposures of $30 million in the case of the

3 See also *Business Review Weekly*, 5 April 1985, 53-54; 2 August 1985, 113; 3 April 1987, 117-8.

NSC were second only to the $104 million loss of the State Bank of Victoria.

Questions began to be asked about the soundness of a bank that figured prominently in the two most serious cases of financial mismanagement. The State Bank had a close relationship with Equiticorp, reinforced by a personal friendship between the State Bank's General Manager, Tim Marcus Clark, and Equiticorp's Alan Hawkins, which stemmed from the days when they both worked for the Commercial Bank of Australia. When Equiticorp collapsed the financial press reported that the exposure of the State Bank group was over $100 million.[4] (*Age*, 15 February 1989, 25) These loans were made despite Equiticorp having no current audited accounts. (*Business Review Weekly*, 27 January 1989, 22-25) It was also revealed that neither the State Bank nor the State Bank of Victoria had any security for their loans to the NSC. This was even more astonishing, given that the accounts for the NSC had been subject to qualification by its auditors. (*Australian Financial Review,* 4 May 1989, 4) What did this suggest about the quality of the State Bank loan book? As Robert Gottliebsen and Mike Debbie noted at the time:

> [T]he ease with which the Safety Council's Victorian Division and Equiticorp were able to raise money from the two banks and other financiers has caused alarm bells to ring in the banking community.
>
> *Business Review Weekly*, 31 March 1989, 29

These events stimulated the critical interest of the Opposition for the first time. However, the Bank and the government were able to assuage the doubts in the mind of the local community. Clark presented a comforting picture in the national press, but those who followed the Bank must have been alarmed at the apparent confusion over the future. In a *Business Review Weekly* interview entitled "State Bank of SA trims its ambitions", Clark stated the belief that at $13.6 billion in assets the Bank had reached a "critical mass of an adequate size so the current plans were for finetuning and reaching a proper level of profitability". (*Business Review Weekly*, 18 August 1989, 43-47) Yet a month later he told the *Australian Financial Review* the Bank was ready to expand further, including plans to expand into South East Asia. He made light of the Equiticorp and the NSC losses, commenting that all banks make some mistakes. (*Australian Financial Review,* 26 September 1989, 48-9)

By 1990 the financial circumstances of the Bank were disastrous but, as we shall see later, because of poor management information systems, no

4 As we shall see, the total loan was in fact $250 million.

one realised how bad they were. In fact the growth in operations was even faster than before. Total assets grew by almost $3 billion to $23.9 billion in the first four months of 1990/91 financial year. While part of this growth was a result of the completion of building projects to which the bank had been committed, some also was the result of credit being extended to debtors to help them cope with the recession and the fall in property asset prices that had become such a prominent feature of the financial landscape. In such cases good money was being thrown after bad.

In addition it was in 1990 that the bank bought New Zealand's biggest building society, the United Building Society, when the New Zealand economy was practically comatose. Like other New Zealand investments, it was justified as a "counter cyclical investment".

For the first half of 1990 the Bank was given a reprieve from the embarrassing questions and revelations that it had suffered in the previous year. Rumours persisted, however, particularly in light of its heavy exposure in the finance and commercial property sectors which were finally suffering from the federal government's high interest rate policy. In May questions were raised in the local media and parliament regarding the Bank's liability for the Myer-REMM project, a huge retail development in the central business district that was plagued with industrial problems. Over the next two months a trio of announcements put the Bank under pressure. A loss of $21.5 million was announced by its major subsidiary, Beneficial Finance, it was found necessary to inject $40 million into the newly acquired but obviously troubled Oceanic Capital Corporation, and then in August the Bank itself announced a plunge in reported profits from $90 million for the previous year to $24 million for 1990-91.

Over the next few months the Bank was embattled. It had to respond to calls for privatisation, to claims of extravagance on the part of its executives, to claims that it had established over 58 off-balance sheet companies, of which even the Premier was not aware, and finally, in December of rumours of large losses about to surface. Its responses became increasingly confused and unconvincing, but the holiday season intervened and so South Australians were stunned with the 10 February announcement that a review commissioned by the Bank by the investment bankers JP Morgan had revealed the need for a government injection of $1 billion to keep the Bank afloat. But as shocking as this was, it was merely the first instalment.

Relationships

In attempting to explain how all the checks and monitoring failed to prevent disaster, we will start by looking at the management of the bank itself and then examine the role of the board, the auditors, the Reserve Bank, the Treasurer and his department and then the parliament. But we should also consider the media and the broader community, for although the political process demands scapegoats, in truth those scapegoats were products of their times and the community that put them there.

Management

During the passing of the *State Bank Bill* several members of parliament referred to the vital importance of the appointment of the chief executive. This was prophetic, for Tim Marcus Clark dominated the events of the next six years.

A Harvard MBA, Tim Marcus Clark came to the State Bank from Westpac. Most of his working life had been in retail organisations. He joined the then Commercial Bank of Australia in 1972. However he had no branch banking experience, nor indeed any "mainstream" banking experience, because his position at the CBA was General Manager, Subsidiaries and Affiliates. (Auditor-General, vol X, 21.16) As one interviewee noted in a 1985 review of management resources, Clark "was not so strong in banking, but as a retailer he was fantastic". (quoted, Auditor-General, vol X, 21.16)

However, the main attraction for the committee established to make the appointment was his role in the merger of the CBA and the Bank of New South Wales to form Westpac. His reputation had been built in the area of organisational change and as such, he was ideal for a government wanting to merge two banks into a new one, with a totally different identity to either of the former components.

One of the key challenges of the new management was to change the organisational culture of the merged entity. The existing culture was widely regarded as staid and paternalistic; not at all suited for the deregulated, high-technology environment of the 1980s.[5]

5 While this was the conventional wisdom at the time, the conservatism of the previous regime is not without question. The impression does not fit well with the fact that the Savings Bank was Australia's first Bank to introduce the payment of interest on personal cheque accounts.

Efforts to change the culture were very successful. Indeed the State Bank experience has been a textbook study in this regard.[6] Senior management was almost completely replaced. Human resources management policies were overhauled. Senior staff were changed. By 1989, only four of the 21 senior officers had had more than 10 years with the Bank. (South Australia, Auditor-General vol X, Appendix B) Only two of the eight-person executive committee in 1984 were still on the committee in 1990 – and one of these was Mr Clark. (Auditor-General, vol X, Appendix C)

Clark was a classically successful executive of the 1980s. Through outstanding leadership, he unified the staff behind the mission he embodied. Clark's enthusiastic, dynamic personality was projected onto staff, steam-rolling dissent and engendering enthusiastic loyalty. It fitted the times; entrepreneurial, risk taking and aggressively oriented to growth.

However, although the implementation of corporate change was very successful – the organisation certainly did change – the design and direction of this process had serious flaws which would eventually create disaster.

The first flaw was a lack of realism. While it is true that optimists make the best salesmen, optimism in dealing with other people's money is a dangerous thing. The senior management's optimism in dealing with other people's money was indicated in the rationale presented to the board for taking over the stockbroker, SVB Day Porter:

> [T]he partners of Day Porter are risk averse. This is a positive quality where comfort is required in relation to the Bank's image of financial prudence but it can also be a negative where new and desirable initiatives remain unfulfilled. Simply put, the Executive Directors of Day Porter continue to think and act as partners. They have personal capital at stake, and have difficulty in coming to terms with the Bank's bigger thinking approach.
>
> South Australia, Royal Commission, 2nd Report, 117,

The Bank's approach to getting business reflected Clark's optimism that the economy would go on growing and asset prices would not fall. Loans issued would be repaid, to the Bank's profit. Because the risk factor was discounted, the Bank could issue loans faster and more favourably than its competitors.

The second flaw was a lack of adequate control measures. With Clark's optimism, combined with an emphasis on selling rather than managing, it is not surprising that control measures in the bank were poor, sometimes astonishingly so. Strategic plans and short term profit plans

---

6 This has been the subject of a teaching case study. See Patrickson and Dawson, 1994.

were prepared but they bore little relationship to reality throughout the history of Clark's stewardship. (Figure 2.2)

Figure 2.2: Planned growth according to strategic plans, compared with actual growth

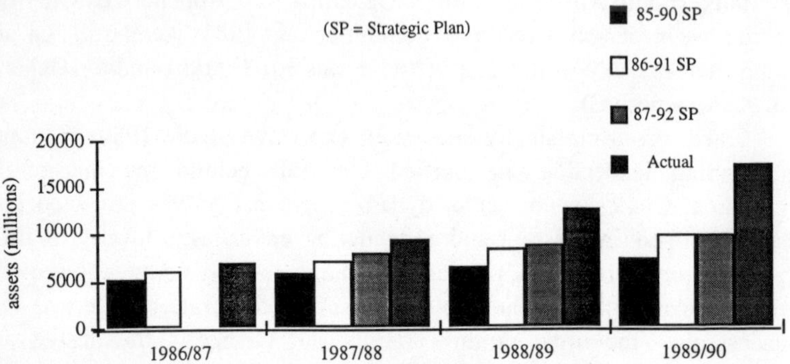

(source: Royal Commission, Second report, pp. 57, 103)

Growth by 1990 was three times that planned in 1985. Subsequent plans attempted, but failed, to catch up with reality. Profit, on the other hand, was almost always less than predicted in absolute terms and always less than predicted when expressed as a return on assets. But even the relatively modest profit figures were inflated by "profit enhancement" measures, most notably a serious under provisioning for bad debts. (eg, Royal Commission, First Report, 242-3)

But the important point to note, of course, is that growth continually *exceeded* expectations. This was regarded, both within the Bank and outside of it, as a cause for congratulations. However in a world in which growth was only limited by the ability to find equally reckless customers (which in the 1980s was not difficult) such growth was really no difficulty.[7]

The variation between achievement and plan should have been seen as an indictment of the ability of the management to control the organisation.

---

7 The lack of constraint is demonstrated in this remarkable passage from the 1984-85 Profit Plan:

> "[T]he Bank will lend as much money as borrowers seek, provided that it is at market rates of interest". (quoted, Royal Commission, 2nd Report, 37)

Of course the qualification regarding market rates of interest was interpreted very liberally.

The plans bore so little relation to reality it would be fair to say the Bank did not plan at all.

This was particularly apparent after the 1987 stock market crash. This sobering experience led senior management to declare the goal of the 1987-88 Profit Plan to be "profitability at the expense of growth". Clark for once was pessimistic about the future, reporting to the board in November 1987 that the Bank was heading into "very difficult times which will not correct quickly"; that the Bank faced the prospect of "customers getting into financial difficulties, increasing non-accrual accounts, increasing bad debts and challenges in meeting our lending targets with high quality loans". (quoted, Royal Commission, First Report, 132) In that year assets actually grew 40%! (Royal Commission, First Report, 162)

Strategic plans were simply a ritual for board and public consumption. They were routinely ignored by management. The 1989-94 strategic plan is a clear example of how far such plans could be divorced from reality. It based its expectations of growth not on previous growth, but on growth predicted in previous plans. It predicted future growth to be 20% per year, compounded, yet a few months later Clark was publicly stating that the Bank was now going to consolidated, because "We now have a critical mass of adequate size". (Royal Commission, Second Report, 154-5)

For most of the time it seems the plans were designed only to give an appearance of a well-run organisation, yet at the end it appears as if Clark really thought they meant something. By May 1990 when both senior management and the board were coming to terms with reality and neither had the heart for trying to speculate what things would be like four years hence, Clark insisted on the production of a strategic plan which was the most fantastic of all. It envisaged growth of 11% per annum, and what is more amazing, when profits were about to dip to practically break even levels, it predicted profit compounding at 30% over the next four years. (Royal Commission, First Report, 350) This was despite the past record and despite present disasters. At this point the comparison with Hitler in the bunker, commanding non-existent armies, is irresistible.

Growth was always higher than expected because the organisational culture and financial incentives were always heavily weighted in favour of writing new business and against prudence. There was not a policy manual on credit risk management until 1988. (Auditor-General, vol 1, 1.29) It was not until 1989 that the Bank seriously set about creating a management information system that would identify the extent of its bad and doubtful loans.

Internal audit was seriously inadequate for the first five years at least. Soothing words to the financial press about "roving internal audit squads" to keep quality of loans high (*Australian Business*, 10 June 1987, 105) masked a reality later described by the head of internal audit:

> [I]n the first years – at least three years – it was just a battle to stay afloat for the organisation because of the large, unprecedented – astronomical growth and totally inadequate system.
>
> Quoted, Auditor-General, vol 1, 1.108)

Until 1989 at least, the internal audit function lacked an appropriate methodology, it could not get access to necessary information, and it lacked both resources and expertise. Until 1988 the function had no qualified accountants. (Auditor-General vol XI, 23.61) For the first few years the internal audit section did not keep pace with the changing nature of the Bank, confining its activities to the traditional role of checking retail activities in the local branches. Head office activities, such as corporate banking, were ignored. (Auditor-General vol XI, 23.14) Overseas activities were particularly poorly served by internal audit. The London office was not examined by internal audit from its opening in 1985 to April 1989, by which time it had over $1b in assets. (Auditor-General vol XI, 23.30)

It was an internal "self-audit" that identified these problems, not senior management. The internal audit function suffered from the indifference and even the hostility of senior management. In keeping with the low priority to which it was assigned, internal audit was not responsible to the General Manager, but instead to a Divisional Manager who was himself a potential auditee. (Auditor-General vol XI, 23.19) The hostility increased after the appointment of a audit supervisor for head office operations in late 1988. The new appointee, clearly disturbed by what she found, soon ruffled feathers with her enquiries and reports. (Auditor-General vol XI, 23.20ff) In September 1990, a few months before the horrendous losses became public, the Chief General Manager, Australian Banking, "warned off" the internal audit section; in regard to credit and pricing issues:

> I would wish to sound a word of caution that I will most strongly resist the intrusion of Group Audit into areas which I believe are the proper province of management.
>
> I will not contemplate Group Audit intruding on Australian Banking divisional management's responsibilities by seeking, offering, or attempting to influence operational responsibility allocation or judgement about appropriateness or assignment of duties or functions.
>
> Quoted, Auditor-General vol XI, 23.38

To over-optimism and lack of control we should add a third flaw – incompetence. Like all Australian banks, the State Bank found it difficult to gain the necessary expertise to cope with the deregulated and rapidly expanding and rapidly changing finance industry. But it found it more difficult than most because it grew more quickly than most and changed more completely than most. This was most apparent in the new areas:

> The Bank's Corporate Lending business was incompetently conducted in almost every respect, from the procedures used in initiating loan proposals to the approval of loans by the Board of Directors.
>
> Auditor-General, vol I, 1.22

In the 1980s staff with the necessary financial skills became very valuable. Though it attempted to match the salaries of the big banks, key staff at the State Bank were notable for their inexperience, particularly in dealing with the full economic cycle. That is, few had had any experience dealing with an economic downturn. The former trading bank was relatively small and so there were few existing staff with much experience in the new activities. But those that had such experience were overlooked or pensioned off as they did not fit the new corporate culture. In fact such was the difficulty in obtaining staff in the Treasury Division that it eventually partly located in Sydney in order to attain the necessary skills and experience. (Auditor-General, vol I, 1.45)

Clark moulded the Bank in his own image through the recruitment of staff, the rewards provided and the creation of an organisational culture with a powerful socialising influence. His vision, his leadership, blanketed opposition. Senior staff would act in accordance with what they perceived he wanted. Ironically this vision was never formally expressed in any strategic plan, but it was known well enough. It was articulated by a former board chairman in a later interview with the Auditor-General, when he described Clark as "a very aggressive, entrepreneurial chap, keen to see the Bank do well . . . keen to see the State Bank with Tim Marcus Clark become Australia's number one bank". (quoted, Auditor-General, vol X, 21.18)

External audit

If the Bank's internal processes were not capable of providing the necessary checks, what about the external auditors?

First of all, it is important to note that the Bank was not audited by the State Auditor-General. Parliament followed the popular trend to have government-owned enterprises operate as much as possible like a privately-owned company, by not having it subject to the Auditor-General. The Bank's Act required the board to appoint two or more company auditors who were required, inter alia, to give their opinion as to whether the accounts were properly drawn up and "give a true and fair view of the matters to which they relate". Private sector auditors operate under the companies legislation and audit requirements under this legislation are not as intensive as those required of the Auditor-General.[8] More detailed assessment is required in a public audit and, perhaps most importantly, the Auditor-General reports to the parliament. The client of the private auditor, by contrast, is the board of the company. When combined with the fact that private sector auditors must compete for business, we have only the professional ethics of the auditors to counter the self-interest of simply providing the information the board wants to hear, whether or not that is in the interests of the ultimate owners of the company. As the Senate Committee on Finance and Public Administration notes, this problem is only compounded when the private auditor also has significant other business with the client, such as management consultancy, which could be threatened by an unpopular report. (Senate Standing Committee on Finance and Public Administration 1989, 36)

To this inherent difficulty we should add the fact that auditing firms faced the same problems as the banks in attracting and retaining staff needed to cope with finance industry that was both expanding and changing. When criticised by the Auditor-General for providing inappropriate and inadequate audits from 1985 to 1990 and so failing to prevent the overstating of profits, KPMG's Executive Chairman responded by saying that the Auditor-General's report appeared to have been "prepared by people with little appreciation of the economic conditions or the business situation of the time". (*Advertiser*, 1 July 1993, 2)

The auditors used were Touche Ross and KPMG Peat Marwick. The major subsidiary, Beneficial Finance, was audited by Price Waterhouse. All three were criticised by the Auditor-General for inadequate reporting, including failing to note misleading and false information and, in the case of Price Waterhouse, failing to note the effect of BFC's off balance sheet companies on group accounts. (Auditor General, vol XIII, 112-114)

The auditors did raise issues of concern in their reports to the State Bank board. A perennial issue was the level of provisioning for bad debts. However, at worst this was described as "at a bare minimum" (quoted,

8 For a discussion of this issue, see Senate Standing Committee on Finance and Administration (1989).

Royal Commission, Second Report, 159), rather that what it was – inadequate, given the risky nature of the business being written and that fact that it was well below the level required by the Reserve Bank.

Also concerns about existing conditions were frequently accompanied by soothing words about measures being taken to address the problems. Perhaps the best example of this is the 1986 report on internal audit capabilities. (Auditor-General, vol XI, 23.51ff) While it would be wrong to say the auditors' report gave a rosy picture, it was certainly far less tough than internal audit's own assessment of a year later. For example in the area of international activities, which had not been addressed at all by internal audit, the report had this to say:

> Progress has been somewhat slower in this department due to the initial lack of proper procedures/ instruction manuals (now in the course of preparation) and the fact that the allocated Internal Auditors were concentrating their attention in the corporate area.
>
> *We will monitor the development of the Internal Audit function in this department to establish that the proposed audit program is adequate* and to ensure that any necessary amendments to documentation and the program are effected.
>
> Quoted, Auditor-General, vol ll, 23.52 [emphasis added]

While some allowance should be made for the fact that Bank staff may not have been as frank as they should have been with the auditors, the Auditor-General's comment should also be noted: "There is no evidence of the external auditor's monitoring the Internal Audit department in this respect". (Auditor-General, vol XI, 23.52)

It is also very surprising that the value of the assets as referred to in the audited statements of June 1990 could be so different when assessed by JP Morgan a few months later.

The State Bank Board

The *State Bank of South Australia Act* places responsibility for the governance of the Bank in the board. It was to administer the Bank's affairs with a view to promoting the "balanced development of the state's economy" and "the maximum advantage to the people of the state, and shall pay due regard to the availability of housing loans". The board was further instructed to administer the Bank "in accordance with accepted principles of financial management and with a view to achieving a profit". (s 15)

Board control of public enterprises has always been difficult. One problem is that government-appointed boards frequently reflect the multiple aims with which the enterprise is invested and so will reflect interests rather than expertise. Second, they will often be squeezed between the personalities and the concerns of the minister and the chief executive officer. Third, without the discipline of tense shareholder's meetings and one's own position and reputation being on the line, there is not the incentive to be assertive even if it is felt to be in the best interests of the enterprise and its owners.

Though most members had a commercial background, they simply did not have the experience to control a bank of the sort the State Bank was to become. In fact, apart from Clark, none had bank management experience. Collectively they represented some of the leading names in Adelaide's business and government circles, but this was not good enough to control a bank operating globally and on many fronts.

As it turned out, the vital qualities needed were as much in terms of personality as expertise. The first chairman of the new Bank was later to recall the report of the executive search agency which brought Tim Marcus Clark to the board's attention. (Royal Commission, First Report, 34). If they wanted a entrepreneur, he was the man. One of his referees noted, however, he would need to be restrained from giving full rein to his entrepreneurial ideas. Unfortunately putting a halter on Clark was not easy. Clark's strong, persuasive personality dominated board meetings.

In 1989 the government made several appointments which it could have reasonably assumed to provide an effective counter to Clark. Both Mr David Simmons (the new chair) and Mr Rod Hartley had reputations as strong, successful businessmen. And yet such assumptions proved ill-founded. Though board meetings became more tense as the Bank's financial position became more apparent, the board still capitulated to Clark in a way described by the Royal Commissioner as "almost bizarre". (Royal Commission, Second Report 199) (Perhaps most bizarre was the 34% pay increase to senior management in August 1990, when mismanagement of disastrous proportions was becoming plain to see.)

Clark was later to be scathing about the quality of the board of which he was a member, telling the Royal Commission that it was inept, badly led and among other things, that it "failed in its duty to exercise proper supervision and control over the CEO". (quoted, Royal Commission, Second Report, 202)

From the start the board adopted a passive approach, simply approving or not approving reports and recommendations put to it by the management. From time to time it commissioned reports from management but if these were not forthcoming, it did not insist. It was not until too late that it took the initiative to insist on the implementation of remedies to perceived defects. Reviews in 1987 and 1989 revealed defects in lending practices, but in both cases the board was assured by management that steps were being made to remedy the situation. (Royal Commission, Second Report, 154)

There is no doubt that the board was badly informed. Reports were frequently not presented in a form that allowed a busy person to get to the kernel of the matter. Sometimes important information, for example Reserve Bank concerns, was simply not conveyed. Other information was misleading. Yet on occasions when it did receive warning signs it did not take adequate action. It allowed itself to be rushed into decisions, sometimes using the "round robin" procedure of having each director contacted individually without the chance to discuss the matter collectively. The decision to commit the equivalent of 50% of its net assets in a loan to Equiticorp was handled this way.

Why was the board so reticent? Why did it not confront Clark? Clearly the members did not foresee the seriousness of the situation that would befall them. Clearly also, the concerns they felt about Clark were muted by his public reputation as a corporate hero and particularly by the perception that he was close to the Treasurer. As we shall discuss later, to be seen to be disagreeing with such a high profile executive would be a brave thing to do.

Reserve Bank

Another source of confidence for the South Australian government and parliament was the Reserve Bank. A function of the Reserve Bank is to maintain the integrity of the Australian financial system by ensuring that licensed banks maintain appropriate prudential standards. As a State government body, the State Bank was not under the formal authority of the Reserve Bank. It is true that the State government wanted the Reserve's oversight to extend to the State Bank and in 1984 the State Bank agreed to informal prudential supervision. (Royal Commission, First Report, 379)

It is important to note that without the cooperation of the banks concerned, the Reserve was reliant on the same information as that available to government. For example its information on matters such as the proportion of loans in commercial real estate was provided by State

Bank management. Although the State government "drew comfort" from Reserve Bank supervision, it had little idea of what it involved. Neither Bank reported to the government on the relationship.

Although the State Bank voluntarily agreed to Reserve Bank oversight, the commercial advantage in being *seen* to be doing so is clear in this explanation of the relationship by Clark when interviewed by the Auditor-General:

> We had no legal liability to the Reserve Bank. It was purely an arrangement that was a gentleman's agreement. We had no legal liability or no legal reason to follow any request from the Reserve Bank. Even though that was the legal significance, we certainly didn't act that way. We bent over backwards to try to act as if we were a nationally operating bank fully under the control of the Reserve Bank.
>
> . . . [F]or this reason [public confidence] we are also keen to co-operate with the Reserve Bank to ensure that we are perceived as meeting and maintaining the prudential standards consistent with those of the other banks.
>
> Quoted, Auditor-General, vol VII, 15.177

However it is plain that Clark had little patience for the cautious, "tea-and-scones" approach of the Reserve Bank. Unlike other bank CEOs, he did not attend meetings held between the Reserve and bank officers and was frequently critical of their intrusion. (Royal Commission, First Report, 381)

For several years Clark resisted the Reserve's having direct communication with the State Bank's external auditors. He relented only when the Reserve pointed out that foreign central banks often sought the Reserve's assurance regarding Australian banks establishing branches in their country; that is, the Reserve's blessing would be needed for overseas expansion. (Royal Commission, First Report, 382)

The Reserve Bank felt no sense of responsibility to the owners of the State Bank. It felt it was responsible to the federal government and parliament for the stability of the Australian banking system as a whole – not for individual banks within it. It did not communicate its concerns about individual banks to the owners of these banks. (Royal Commission, First Report, 380)

The most serious rift between the Reserve and the State Bank occurred over the 1987 decision to loan money to Equiticorp. The $250 million involved represented over 50% of the Bank's net assets, well above the 30% limit the Reserve applied to the commercial banks. The Reserve strongly counselled against such an exposure, particularly in light of the fact that Clark himself was a director of Equiticorp. It told bank officers it would have prevented the loan if it had the authority, but did not tell either the State Treasurer or his department. (Royal Commission, First Report, 385) Not only did the management dismiss the Reserve's concerns, they did not even inform the board of them until after it had approved the loan. On another occasion the State Bank at least showed some respect for the Reserve by going to the bother of structuring a deal with the State Government Insurance Corporation in order to abide by the letter (though not the spirit) of Reserve Bank guidelines. (Royal Commission, First Report, 197)

Having no formal authority over the Bank, the Reserve had to rely on persuasion and the weight of its position to convince the management, the board and the government of the need for due care. Yet very often its views were not passed on to the board, the Treasury or the Treasurer. For example, its concern regarding the Equiticorp loan was not conveyed to the Treasury. Even when the board was appraised of Reserve Bank concerns, these were not passed onto the government. (Royal Commission, First Report, 385)

At one stage the Reserve realised that its messages to State Bank officers were not being accurately conveyed to the board, yet it took "no action beyond a very gentle and soft comment" to the Bank. (Royal Commission, First Report, 384)

The first State Bank Royal Commissioner put down the Reserve's attitude to "aloofness":

> The Reserve Bank perceived the incipient problems of the Bank at least as early as 1987, but it must have been aware that its views often went unheeded by the Bank; in failing so to inform the Government it was guided by its policy of aloofness for the shareholder-owners of the banks for which it had a statutory responsibility. However, it was neither logical nor commercially and financially sensible to adopt the same policy of aloofness from the owner of a State bank which had voluntarily submitted to its surveillance.
>
> Royal Commission, First Report, 392

The Minister

Next in the chain of accountability and control is the minister; in this case the Treasurer and Premier, John Bannon. From the time the losses were first announced in February 1991 until his resignation as Premier in August 1992 the responsibility of the Premier for the disaster was the main concern of State politics.

The dominant feature of the Treasurer's oversight of the Bank was a desire to give the Bank the freedom it needed to operate in the commercial environment.

As we shall see, the view that the Bank should be left free to pursue its commercial judgement had ample support in the parliamentary debate over the *State Bank Bill*. The Royal Commissioner summed up his impression of the feelings of the time this way:

> The universal hubris surrounding its conception and birth reflected the expectation that it could, and should, be free of Government pressures . . . and not be subject to Government prescription.
>
> Royal Commission, First Report, 47

As the Royal Commissioner also noted, the Treasurer and the Treasury therefore had plenty of justification for a "hands off" approach, at least in the early years. It could be argued that such a policy was endorsed until the collapse of Equiticorp and the National Safety Council. But to continue this policy, after these episodes, without even tightening the monitoring of the Bank, was certainly not sanctioned by parliament.

Bannon relied on the board to undertake its statutory responsibilities and on the Reserve Bank to ensure prudent behaviour. Perhaps most of all, he relied on Tim Marcus Clark, for whom he had a very high regard. Throughout the 1980s Clark was a feather in the government's cap, lauded by the national financial and local media. As a politician, Mr Bannon both shared this enthusiasm and was concerned about the political implications of any undermining of Clark's position. His high regard for the managing director led him to accept Clark's explanations of apparently poor profit levels. For example, Bannon accepted Clark's argument that it was necessary to have fine margins between borrowing and lending rates to establish a market. Profits would eventually come.

The loyalty that Clark obtained, both within the Bank and within the government, was to some extent created by Clark's ability to present information that they wanted to hear. Over optimistic forecasts combined with bland dismissal of discordant evidence to convince most that all was going well. Clark's subterfuge was supported by a deep desire by everyone – the government, the Bank's staff, the media, the community as a whole – to *want* it to go well. Bannon was no different.

But to say that the Premier simply reflected the hopes of the community he led is not to excuse him. The *State Bank Act* and the conventions of parliamentary democracy placed him in an important position of responsibility to ensure that the Bank was acting in the State's best interests. In trying to deal with the dilemma between commercial freedom and ultimate political accountability and control the balance was tipped too much toward the former.

At times the "hands-off" approach was jettisoned when political fortunes required it. The clearest (but in financial terms the most trivial) example was the pressure put on the Bank to forestall housing interest rate rises at the 1987 federal and 1985 and 1989 State elections. The amounts of foregone revenue were small, a few million or so, and in fact the ALP made no secret of its role, believing action to keep interest rates down was a vote winner. It was freely reported in the media that Bannon was willing to accept a lower profit as a result. (Royal Commission, First Report, 87)

A more serious (but more subtle) intervention concerned the Myer-REMM retail complex. The project, involving over a half a billion dollars, was touted as the biggest retail project in the country and portrayed in the local media as both a "saviour" of Rundle Mall and a test of the State's ability to attract major construction projects. Always finely balanced, the project became the State Bank's biggest single loss. The board knew that the Premier was keen to see the project go ahead "if it was commercially feasible" but Bannon later told the Royal Commission that he would have been disappointed if the board approved it because the government wanted it to. (*Advertiser*, 21 August 1992, 6) Nevertheless the Royal Commissioner concluded that the activities of the Bank in its dealings with State government officials who were keen to see the project go ahead "reflects explicitly" that the Bank was not fully independent. (Royal Commission, First Report, 202) Bannon's role in this was not active, but as the representative of the Bank's owners he should have been a force on the side of caution.

Perhaps the most serious involvement of the Treasurer in the Bank's affairs was his attitude to Tim Marcus Clark. His regard for Clark and the board's perception of this have been referred to earlier. Relations between Clark and the rest of the board deteriorated from early 1989 when it became more and more obvious that despite promises, little had been done to improve management defects identified earlier and the losses over Equiticorp and the National Safety Council revealed the dangers of the Clark style. By 1990 it appears most members of the board were ready to dismiss the CEO but felt unable to do so because of the concerns of the Treasurer. In October 1990 Bannon told senior members that he thought the removal of Clark would be "unwise", but he would accept any decision they made. (Royal Commission, First Report, 370) Of course by 1990 the chickens had taken flight and were on their way home to roost – nothing could save the Bank from massive losses. But earlier remedial action would have lessened the losses and such action was only taken after Clark resigned.

To be fair to Premier Bannon the signals he was getting from the board were not clear. Some individuals were using backdoor means to make him aware of their concerns but in the absence of clear concurrence from the chairman, the Premier was entitled to regard such expressions as due to personality clashes. The board itself never conveyed any concern about the management of the Bank. It was not until July 1990 that the chairman demurred from Clark's increasingly absurd assurances during the regular meetings with the Treasurer. Bannon was warned of possible losses as early as mid-1989, but preferred to accept the official accounts and reports by Clark and the chairman. By July 1990 Premier Bannon was being warned by the chairman that there would be losses and by September the contradictory statements by Clark had caused Bannon to lose faith in the Bank's account of the circumstance. But his refusal to order an inquiry into the Bank was based on the reasonable belief that any losses would be "manageable" (at that time $200 million was about the worst figure to reach his ears) and that any announcement of an inquiry would itself harm the Bank and the State's economy. For the same reason he was reluctant to give his blessing to Tim Marcus Clark's removal.

Though seen in this light Premier Bannon's position is understandable, he bore a heavy burden of responsibility for allowing the situation to develop. In a sense the failure of the Bank was a failure of an ideology which Bannon subscribed to. The ideology was a misreading of the commercial world, for in seeking to give the Bank as much autonomy as possible to act in a commercial manner, Bannon did not realise that commercial companies are normally constrained by anxious shareholders, willing and able to divest themselves if they feel the company is not acting in their interest. As the Royal Commissioner noted, the Treasurer did not himself take a commercial perspective in his ownership role; it was not in his nature to take that approach. (Royal Commission, First Report, 208) This view has been endorsed by the head of the Department of Premier and Cabinet throughout this period, Mr Guerin:

> I think John Bannon was fundamentally a politician; a person who deals with public issues and policy. Although he had a reasonable grasp of economics, he's no economist. He's not a financier and he's not a top rate practical manager; you don't expect premiers to have all those qualities.
>
> Quoted, Kenny 1993, 129

Though required under the *State Bank Act* to give approval for major acquisitions Bannon rarely had the necessary information to make a real decision. Of course ministers normally rely on briefings from their departments in making decisions, but in this case the hands-off approach extended to the Treasury's dealings with the Bank as well.

Bannon did not encourage Treasury interest, even to the point of not requiring a briefing for his regular meetings with the Bank. (Royal Commission, First Report 79, 251) On those occasions when it did express concerns they were not acted upon by the Treasurer. Neither did he support Treasury's long campaign to have a representative, or at least an observer, at board meetings. Even the argument that Treasury could not advise on appointments to the board without knowledge of performance on the board did not convince him.

It is understandable that Treasury should interpret this as meaning it should not assign a high priority to its monitoring of the Bank, particularly given that under the "hairshirt" policy of the central agencies, Treasury lost significant staff resources during this period. Besides, Treasury officials were being told in a review of the public service that they were to adopt a "no-nonsense management style" emphasising results rather than process, and which, among other things, "is prepared to innovate and take risks".[9] Prudential oversight of the State's symbol of entrepreneurialism was obviously not required. It was frequently pressured to give quick advice regarding purchases and felt that unless it could give clear evidence why a purchase should not proceed it would be wrapping it in red tape to say wait.

One would have expected a change of behaviour after the revelations of early 1989, once the Bank became politically contentious. Treasury officials clearly were losing faith in the Bank's pronouncements. But little of this reached the Premier. The 1989-92 strategic plan was criticised, but toward the end the cynicism seems to have manifested itself in quiescence. Profit plans that had formerly been subject to critique now went without comment, despite being even less realistic. The Under-Treasurer did not challenge predictions given to Bannon that he knew to be rubbish. (Royal Commission, First Report, 323)

One can imagine the sighs with which Treasury set about the task of "cashing up" in preparation for a downgrading of the State's credit rating that would result from the announcement of major losses. This began in September 1990. The Treasurer was not told it was doing so.

---

9 South Australia, Review of Government Management (1983), 9.

Parliament

Parliament has the crucial role in ensuring the executive is accountable to the people. But in this case there were several impediments to it being able to do so. Most obviously there was simply a lack of adequate information or expertise to understand such information. It has taken major reports of the Auditor-General and a Royal Commission, each costing many millions of dollars and with very extensive powers of investigation, to explain what went wrong. What hope did parliament have, with little expertise, little time to analyse information provided and in any case being denied the information on grounds of "commercial confidentiality"?

In any case until 1989 parliament had little motivation to look carefully into the affairs of the Bank. If anything the debate over the *State Bank Bill* in 1983 revealed an Opposition even more enthusiastic about a bold, entrepreneurial Bank than the government. The Leader of the Opposition took some delight in pointing out that he had urged the merger eight months earlier in his address in reply speech, and that the merger was contrary to ALP policy, which referred to the continuation of separate boards (*SAPD,* 29 November 1983, 2031, 22 March 1983, 523).

In fact it is in Opposition speeches that we see the beginnings of themes which were to characterise the Bank. Several speakers had visions beyond those of the government. They foresaw the Bank growing in size to match those of the recently merged private banks, offering a wide range of services, playing a key role in arranging overseas financing for South Australian development. The Leader of the Opposition noted that:

> Following a world-wide trend for banks to increase in size, market share and size are extremely important in the Australian banking sector. Size is of crucial importance in exposure to major corporate and Government customers and the development of . . . major resource projects.
>
> *SAPD*, 29 November 1983, 2034

Another speaker noted opportunities for growth overseas, welcoming offices in Asia and America, to add to that already existing in London (*SAPD*, 6 December 1983, 2359) Another Opposition spokesperson in Council hoped for an eastern States banker from the private sector to be appointed as CEO to develop international and corporate financing. (*SAPD* 6 December 1983, 2359)

The period from the passing of the Bill in 1983 to 1989 showed very little interest on the part of parliament. One searches in vain for references to the Bank in the indexes of Hansard. Once or twice there are references to a local member's concern that the Bank's interstate activities were detracting from those in South Australia, but that is all. (*SAPD*, 26 February 1985, 3032-3) Annual Reports went unremarked upon. This is less surprising given that parliamentarians usually rely on the Auditor-General's views on financial accounts and in this case there were none.

This changed in early 1989, when Jennifer Cashmore was appointed the Opposition's economics spokesperson. This appointment coincided with the collapse of Equiticorp. In fact Cashmore's first question in parliament as spokesperson concerned the exposure to Equiticorp. The government used what was to become the familiar argument of commercial confidentiality to block the questions. Government responses ridiculed the Opposition for putting a woman with obviously no expertise in charge of such a complex portfolio (*SAPD*, 4 April 1989, 2567-8). It took intimidation tactics a step further by using its numbers in the House of Assembly to pass a censure motion on the Opposition for the "grossest economic vandalism" in daring to question such an important South Australian institution. Cashmore's response – focussing on the need for accountability, questioning the arm's length approach and arguing that the essential accounting concern was the quality of assets in a recessed period – proved to be a remarkably accurate targeting of the real concerns (*SAPD*, 13 April 1989, 3014-9).

Concern was voiced again, later in 1989, when it was suggested that the State Bank had a $40 million dollar exposure in the collapse of Hookers. More alarming was the suggestion from the Leader of the Australian Democrats, Ian Gilfillan, that exposure to bad developments around Adelaide was close to $1 billion (*SAPD* 5 September, 89, 657). When he issued a statement on the matter, the State Bank's response was to sue for libel.

In the second half of 1990 Clark wrote to the Leader of the Opposition, Dale Baker, talking of the damage being caused to innocent South Australians by its actions. The letter, which the Liberals claimed was drafted in the Premier's office, was made public in parliament by the government. (Kenny 1993, 25). It had the effect of putting pressure on the Opposition – their economic irresponsibility became the political issue. Cashmore has since revealed that she received a series of communications from business leaders criticising her for undermining confidence in the State.[10] At the end of 1989 she was removed from her position and the Opposition once again went silent on the State Bank.

---

10 This has been revealed on a number of occasions, for example, ABC *7.30 Report*, Adelaide edition, 7 June, 1993.

But rumours persisted and in May 1990 the Opposition took up the issue again, this time focussing on the Myer-REMM development. As we noted in our brief history above, the next few months provided plenty of material for further questioning. The government adopted the same tactics as before – blocking questions with claims of commercial confidentiality, criticising the Opposition for economic recklessness. Here is a response Clark provided to a question in September 1990, when things were so serious that the board quietly ordered JP Morgan to undertake the fateful review:

> With reference to the question regarding details of loans in property investments, we do not consider it appropriate to provide this information.
>
> Similarly, we consider it inappropriate to reply to the request to provide detailed accounts of every individual company that makes up the State Bank Group.
>
> Enclosed is a copy of our Annual Report which has been audited by two independent auditors and I believe this should be sufficient information for the Leader of the Opposition.
>
> Royal Commission, First Report, 368

At no stage did the government admit the legitimacy of Opposition questions. Nor did it order the inquiry the Opposition was demanding. On the face of it it seems parliament did not perform the function required of it, though no doubt it had a part to play in keeping the heat on the Bank, finally forcing it to order the review. But by then it was three billion dollars too late.

Community

It may be trite to say it, but the government could take the high-handed approach it did to parliament because it was politically expedient to do so. In common with parliaments throughout Australia, South Australia's State parliament was not held in high esteem, either by the government or by the public in general. As Kenny notes, while the South Australian public were not particularly impressed with the Bannon Labor government, particularly after 1985, the Opposition was even less inspiring. He quotes the head of the Department of Premier and Cabinet on the relationship between cabinet members and the parliament:

> They weren't really under too much pressure. I can remember sitting through year after year of budgetary examinations with the parliamentary committees, wondering why on earth these people were wasting their time.
>
> Kenny 1993, 135

The public and the media were so cynical about the point-scoring of the Opposition that when it really did cry wolf it was not believed.

But it was not simply the low esteem in with the Opposition was held that allowed the government's parliamentary tactics to work. More importantly was the high esteem in which the State Bank was held. As has been noted, the rapid growth in the Bank was simply a reflection of the management's inability to manage a plan. But this was not how it was seen by the government, the parliament and the wider community. The faster the growth, the greater the pride in the Bank. This was a time when financial adventurism was uncritically valued, when the media made heroes of all the financial entrepreneurs. How much harder would it be to criticise a hero of the local variety, particularly one working for the people of South Australia?

Throughout the 1980s the media helped generate an uncritical enthusiasm for the Bank within the community as a whole. It was a Bank of which we were all proud, as the Royal Commissioner noted, it was promoted as the "flagship" of the State (*Report*, 22). Journalist Chris Kenny has expressed the feelings of the time this way:

> The State Bank was a way for SA to be great. To attack it was to attack the Festival, or the Crows, or fritz. Uncertain and uncomfortable about its place in the world, this city and its media were a little too eager to enjoy the bank's success.
>
> Kenny 1993, 49

"The only bank with its heart in South Australia" also played an important role in stopping "foreign" (ie, interstate) takeovers of South Australian firms such as Bennett and Fisher and SA Brewing. The Bank was a good news story the South Australian community wanted to believe, and Premier Bannon tapped this public sentiment well when he dismissed the Opposition by saying:

> It is the people's bank – owned by you, me and every other South Australian – which, although it is performing for us, is being undermined and attacked by members opposite.
>
> *SAPD*, 14.2.89, 1878

Marcus Clark was treated with something akin to adulation. A simple after lunch speech about restrictions on development could spark two weeks of concern in the media about our negative approach to planning issues. (See various issues of the *Advertiser*, August 1988.) Projects, in particular the Myer-REMM project, were constantly being touted as "saviours" and a "litmus test" of whether the government could attract the necessary capital to maintain growth. Given the financial millstone that the

REMM-Myer centre was to become, it is ironic to recall an *Advertiser* editorial comment once finance had been secured:

> One of the happiest aspects of the project, after the developers had reported having difficulties getting finance, is that SA's State Bank, headed by Mr Tim Marcus Clark who has recently done much to stimulate the development debate, came to the front by tying together its largest funding package yet for REMM.
>
> The financial go-ahead for this project, and statistical reports of the recent boom in non-residential development in Adelaide, are signs of confidence. This is something we all need to develop.
>
> *Advertiser*, 31 August 1988

The clues for concern about the State Bank first appeared in national newspapers, not the local media. And as we have seen, when the Opposition spokesperson started voicing this concern, she was sharply warned off by senior figures in the local business community. Cashmore has pointed out that through its sponsorships to sport, charities and so on, as well as loans, the Bank "exerted enormous patronage across the length and breadth of the state". (quoted Kenny 1993, 45) According to a senior Treasury official, at no time to his knowledge was the government approached by any member of the business community on a confidential basis suggesting that the Bank's credit controls may be inadequate or the lending approach too risky.

The journalists of the time shared the low opinion of the Opposition and a concern about possible damage to the Bank caused by speculation and questioning.[11] But in some cases they were also subject to intimidation. The *Advertiser's* finance editor was "warned off" by lawyers from the law firm of which the State Bank chairman was senior partner when he ran stories about the Bank's involvement in Equiticorp. He was also denied access to the managing director for about six months. (Kenny 1993, 47) The State Bank's large public relations unit and the Premier's staff denigrated the Opposition. The Bank also resorted to threatening legal action and actually did sue the Leader of the Australian Democrats at one point. The settlement out of court was later publicised by the Premier, though it was meant to be confidential. Also the afternoon *News* was forced to withdraw an item on the Myer-REMM centre due to legal action by the Bank. (Kenny 1993, 48)[12]

---

11 For a discussion of the role of the media in the 1980s, see Kenny, 1993, Chapters 2 and 9.

12 See the *News*, 25 May, for the p 1 apology over REMM.

The media have a symbiotic relationship with their customers. They reflect and reinforce the community parochialism and other values. While individuals want scapegoats and feel frustrated that nobody tells them where the money has gone, so they can get it back, it is important to understand the culpability of the whole community for the financial failures. Although Royal Commissions inevitably take on the flavour of a witchhunt for a few individuals, the blame should be spread much broader. Unfortunately it is very doubtful that this lesson – that the community needs to be more mature in its assessment of its institutions – has been learnt.

References

Gobbett D (1986). The Financial System in Sheridan Kyoko (ed), *The State as Developer: Public Enterprise in South Australia*, Adelaide, Royal Australian Institute of Public Administration, 152-165.

Kenny C (1993). *State of Denial*, Adelaide, Wakefield.

Marshall V (1992). The Labor Party in Parkin A and Patience A, *The Dunstan Decade; the politics of restraint*, Sydney, Allen and Unwin, 36-49.

Parkin A (1992).Looking Back on the Dunstan Decade in Parkin A and Patience A, *The Dunstan Decade; the politics of restraint*, Sydney, Allen and Unwin, 3-24.

Parkin A and Patience A (1992). *The Dunstan Decade; the politics of restraint*, Sydney, Allen and Unwin.

Patience A (1992). The Bannon Decade: Preparation for What? in Parkin A and Patience A, *The Dunstan Decade; the politics of restraint*, Sydney, Allen and Unwin, 343-354.

Patrickson M and Dawson P (1994). State Bank of South Australia in Patrickson M and Bamber G (eds), *Management of Organisational and Industrial Change*, Melbourne, Longman Cheshire (in press).

Scott G (1992). Economic Policy in Parkin A and Patience A, *The Dunstan Decade; the politics of restraint*, Sydney, Allen and Unwin, 71-100.

Senate Standing Committee on Finance and Public Administration (1989). *Government Companies and their Reporting Requirements*, Canberra, AGPS.

South Australia, Auditor-General (1993). *Report of the Auditor-General on an Investigation into the State Bank of South Australia.*

South Australia, Review of Government Management, *Initial Report*, March, 1983.

South Australia, Royal Commission into the State Bank of South Australia, *First Report*, November 1992.

South Australia, Royal Commission into the State Bank of South Australia, *Second Report*, March 1993.

South Australia, Treasury (1992). *South Australian Financial Statement.*

Stokes G (1983). South Australia: Consensus Politics in Parkin A and Warhurst J (eds), *Machine Politics in the Australian Labor Party*, Sydney, Allen and Unwin.

Victoria, *First Report into Royal Commission into the Tricontinental Group of Companies*, July 1991.

Western Australia, *Report of the Royal Commission into Commercial Activities of Government and other Matters, Part II*, November 1992.

3

The Royal Commission Into WA Inc

Allan Peachment

The Opposition parties in Western Australia first demanded the setting up of a Royal Commission into *WA Inc* on 11 August 1989, and by December the Legislative Council was threatening to block supply unless the government acceded. By October 1990 pollsters questions revealed that more than 84% of those interviewed wanted some sort of inquiry into *WA Inc* while 72% wanted a Royal Commission. (*West Australian,* 24 October 1990) After a series of by-election losses for the government the demand for a Royal Commission, linked to a threat to block supply, was again raised this time by both Liberals and Nationals. The new Premier, Carmen Lawrence, again refused arguing that there was an inquiry into Rothwells already underway and that this should be allowed to report. The opposition parties also had their problems and, mainly as a result of dissension on questions of strategy and leadership within Liberal ranks, the Council threat to supply was lifted.[1] Later, in both February and June 1990, the Liberal leader, Barry MacKinnon, introduced a bill into parliament to appoint a wide-ranging Royal Commission into *WA Inc*, a bill which, interestingly, sought to set aside executive privilege, cabinet secrecy or forms of legal privilege.

Calls for a Royal Commission also came from other sources. In August 1990 90 Perth lawyers signed their names to a full page

1 The Labor Party countered the threat to supply by mounting a *Resolution of Parliamentary Disagreements Bill* in the Council which it declared was aimed at reducing the potential for parliamentary chaos and instability resulting from disagreement between the two Houses. The Bill aimed to give the Governor authority to approve supply bills blocked by the Council for more than a month and deadlocks over bills other than supply would be settled by calling a special election to allow voters decide the issue. The measure was defeated. Between 1983 and 1990 the Council had blocked 18 government bills. (*West Australian*, 29 August 1990)

advertisement calling for an inquiry while the protest group, *People for Fair and Open Government*, lead by the Premier's lawyer brother Bevan, received wide media coverage on this and related issues.

Eventually, reversing her previous stance, on 19 November 1990 Premier Lawrence announced the appointment of a Royal Commission into *Commercial Activities of Government and Other Matters*; this began hearings the next March. It is the purpose of this chapter to set down some of the background and operational issues to do with the Commission's inquiries.

The Commission's scope and complexity may be gauged from the facts that over a total of 525 sitting days it heard more than 543 witnesses in 847 appearances, transcribed approximately 50,000 pages of evidence, utilised 4550 exhibits and issued its report in seven volumes. The cost of all this to the public purse was approximately $30 million, $10.6 million of which was paid for the legal representation of past and present politicians and public servants, $2.072 million for former Premier Dowding alone. (*West Australian*, 22 October 1992) Proceedings, which were usually public, were given wide media coverage utilising facilities which set new standards for technical excellence and public access in this field. Its terms of reference required it to inquire into and report on whether there has been corruption, illegal conduct or improper conduct by any person or corporation in the affairs, investment decisions and business dealings of the government of Western Australia or its agencies, instrumentalities or corporations in relation to a wide range of government developments and policies. Three references – (i) natural gas sales agreements, (ii) the Dampier to Perth natural gas pipeline and (iii) Bunbury Foods were all policies associated with the previous Court Liberal government. These references drew minimal public interest and in all three instances the inquiry found that there was no evidence of corrupt, illegal or improper behaviour.

With the remaining references: Halls Head development, Fremantle Anchorage development, Northern Mining Corporation, Burswood Island Casino, Midland Abattoir site, Fremantle Gas and Coke, Swan Building Society, Teachers Credit Society, Rothwells, Central City Properties, Observation City, the Smith and Martin Trial, the adequacy of police investigation, and political donations, the Commission made a number of findings of serious impropriety but, to the astonishment and dismay of many, found that there was comparatively little evidence of illegal or corrupt conduct. However, some confidential evidence was passed to the

Director of Public Prosecutions for consideration with a view to instituting criminal proceedings against unnamed individuals.

The Commission was also directed "to report whether . . . changes in the law of the State, or in administrative or decision making procedures, are necessary or desirable in the public interest". The Commission's response formed Part II of their report, a volume which drew intense interest and much criticism from some commentators.

A series of difficulties were encountered by the Commission in undertaking its task. First, there was the inadequacy, removal and "reconstruction" of records and files of a number of public and private organisations, including the merchant bank Rothwells, the State government Insurance Commission and in some ministerial offices. This obviously raises suspicions of whether a cover-up of corrupt, illegal or improper behaviour had taken place. For example, in the weeks before Brian Burke's retirement as Premier, several members of his staff were engaged in removing and destroying material from departmental files. While this raised suspicions it may well have been an innocent activity. In addition, however, Deputy Premier Parker retained possession of official documents, including originals. (RC[2] 1.1.27, Pt II) Second, there was the Commission's inability to compel the attendance of some witnesses, including the wife of former Deputy Premier David Parker, Kim Rooney, who refused all requests to travel to Perth from Hong Kong to give evidence. A third problem area was the marked lack of recollection of relevant past events on the part of many key witnesses; indeed, a computer check on the number of times the phrase "I can't recall" was used caused the computer to "give up"!

While some hearsay evidence was given, the Commissioners argued that the greater proportion of evidence presented at the inquiry would have been admissible in a civil or criminal court. Addressing their terms of reference, the Commissioners gave particular attention to the interpretation they intended placing on the concepts of "corruption", "illegal conduct" and "improper conduct". "Corruption" was for all intents and purposes taken as being conduct characterised as such in the *Criminal Code.* The Commissioners agreed that "improper conduct" signified, among other things, conduct lacking any legal sanction. Certainly, it was to be expected that, in most cases, improper conduct would be accompanied by an awareness that it was not right, or less than proper, or not the appropriate action in the circumstances, or otherwise open to criticism. Where conduct

2 References to RC indicate Royal Commission, followed by the number of the appropriate paragraph.

was improper by reason of the purpose for which it was undertaken, the Commissioners argued that the pursuit of that purpose would ordinarily, but not necessarily, be accompanied by a consciousness of impropriety. On the other hand, they added, a course of conduct could be undertaken in good faith for what were believed to be desirable ends but yet, on objective analysis, found to have been misconceived as to render the conduct improper. In circumstances where a person may thoughtlessly place themselves in a conflict of interest situation they may be found guilty of improper conduct however, mere negligence or carelessness is unlikely to be characterised as improper. (RC 1.6.57) Agreeing, finally, that the words were somewhat "chameleon-like" the consensus "hammered out" by the Commissioners was that:

> [I]mproper conduct would be established where there was a gross departure from those standards of public administration the public are entitled to expect and which is otherwise inexplicable. An alternative form of words for the final phrase would be "and which defies rational explanation.
>
> RC 1.6.58

None of this was to necessarily imply that if guilty of improper conduct an officer had deliberately abused the authority of his or her position for improper ends. In addition, the Commissioners emphasised that the main body of the report should not be read as if a finding of improper conduct implied a finding of illegal conduct. In the majority of cases they made clear, this would not be so. (RC 1.6.56)

For those who may feel that this definition of improper conduct focused on public servants only, the Commissioners were re-assuring, pointing out that while the measure of responsibility of ministers of the Crown compared with public servants may differ, the conduct itself admits to only one characterisation. (RC 1.6.59) However, the Minister's commitment to openness, accountability, integrity, the public interest and the purpose underlying a course of conduct undertaken or directed by a minister is likely to be very much more relevant. (RC 1.6.59) This is to argue that a minister may be expected and perhaps excused for placing ends above means in implementing policy, whereas the public servant should be expected to pay much greater attention to means, that is, process. This is not only a succinct statement of the largely unwritten codes of behaviour prevailing amongst the great majority in the service but, argued the Commissioners, is a worthy goal in itself.

Parliamentary privilege

In the Western Australian parliament the doctrine of parliamentary privilege is largely determined less by the parliament than by the Speaker, the President and by party leaders. The doctrine's century-long history as set down in the State parliament's 1991 official history by former Clerk of the Legislative Assembly, and co-author Bruce Okely, describes the parliament's actions in respect of matters of privilege as, "less than elegant or at the very least somewhat of an overreaction". (Okely et al 1991, 420) As an illustration, in October 1992 the Labor Speaker, Mike Barnett, warned MPs not to "casually criticise" the way in which he used his casting vote when they were being interviewed by the media as this could jeopardise the privileges of parliament. Normally safely ignored, parliamentary privilege became a major issue at the time of the setting up of the Royal Commission – and again in the post report atmosphere of reform years later – and the topic is therefore worthy of a major diversion in this discussion.

The Commissioners, while mindful of freedom of speech and the need to protect the proceedings of parliament, posed what was by far the most important question of privilege ever dealt with by the State parliament. Arguing that it would assist the proper performance of their task if they were able to scrutinise the statements and conduct of persons who were members of parliament at various times in the 1980s, as well as the testimony of witnesses called before various parliamentary committees on matters relating to the Commission's terms of reference, the Commissioners' requested the presiding officers for a temporary waiver of privilege. Their request was refused on the basis of article 9 of the *Bill of Rights 1689* as written into the 1891 *Parliamentary Privileges Act.*[3] It was revealed years later that neither the Speaker nor the President consulted either their respective Houses or their party leaders before rejecting the Commissioners' request.(*West Australian*, 18 May 1994)

Not to be put off by this rebuff, the Commissioners, having some "disquiet over the breadth of the privilege" claimed by the parliament's presiding officers and clerks, decided to appeal to the power of each house to waive privilege in limited and defined circumstances to do with the

3 The relevant article states: "That the freedom of speech, and debates or proceedings in Parliament, ought not to be impeached or questioned in any court or place out of Parliament".

inquiry.[4] Their suggested resolution, supported by extensive argument was rejected by the President of the Legislative Council, who responded:

> Despite the difficulties that may be encountered in the course of taking evidence as a result of the view I have taken, I am bound to restate, . . . that the Commission is an arm of the Executive Government and I would be very slow, for that reason alone, to concede that art [sic] 9's application to the Commission's proceedings may be removed, no matter how pressing the public interest may be.
>
> RC 1.6.73

This letter was followed two days later by one from two presiding officers who, among other things wrote:

> We have considered your request very carefully but have concluded that even should a contrary opinion be available, it would not persuade us to change our stated view of the matter. In this type of situation, we feel obliged to take account of the precedents and opinions expressed in other Parliaments, particularly the House of Commons and those in Australia.
>
> RC 1.6.74

Given the obeisance paid by the Western Australian parliament to parliaments at Westminster and elsewhere, it is interesting to note that a number of the privileges of the House of Commons have been surrendered over the years. For example, privilege of freedom from arrest has been extinguished, members may also be arrested under emergency powers and a new frame of reference for the House's exercise of its penal jurisdiction has recently been created. (May 1989, 83) Contrary to the arguments of the presiding officers the precedents for minor change already exist at the Commons. There are further precedents available closer to home, for example, the 1989 bicentenary publication on the Commonwealth Parliament lists three recent instances of the use of parliamentary records in court proceedings; in no instance did the parliament take action against the practice. (Reid et al 1989, 293)[5]

---

4 The 21st edition of Erskine May's: *Parliamentary Practice* (p 91) may have a precedent for this, saying, "When in 1980 the Commons gave leave for reference to be made in court proceedings to the Official Report and to the published reports and evidence of committees ... the resolution explicitly reaffirmed the status of proceedings in Parliament confirmed by article IX of the *Bill of Rights*". Perhaps in agreeing to the Commissioners' request a simple reaffirmation was all that was necessary to safeguard the parliament's rights.

5 In correspondence to *West Australian* on 7 May 1994 the President of the Council denied the validity of this example. Perhaps a better example was the innovative way in which the House of Commons Privileges Committee concluded at the beginning of the Second World War that the detention of a Member under Emergency Powers legislation

Not to be deterred by the President's total disregard for the public interest the Commissioners made one final appeal by writing to Premier Lawrence suggesting that the Bill then before the parliament to amend the *Royal Commissions Act 1968* be revised so as to vary the operation of the privilege "to the very limited extent and for the limited purpose proposed". No reply was received. The leader of the National Party, Hendy Cowan, did respond to the Commissioners' plea but declined any support for the idea of amending the Act, as did the Leader of the Opposition, Barry MacKinnon, who supported the views of the Speaker and the President while offering sympathy to the Commissioners.

Journalists pursued the Premier on this question of privilege and her responses to their questions revealed a degree of confusion. In an abridged version of her comments she stated:

> It's clearly a matter for the whole parliament . . . it's got such a long history . . . there probably needs to be a justification . . . if during the Commission people had used the parliament to make statements that could not be challenged by the Commission, I'd be more worried about that. Historical scrutiny is less of a problem and that is what parliament is trying to protect . . . I think everyone agrees that there were other means for them to discover these matters . . . there are times when MPs are guilty of using privilege as a shield against investigation.
>
> *West Australian*, 21 November 1992

As the Commissioners noted, given the parliament had passed the Act creating the Commission in the first place it would seem that the Commission was no longer to be regarded only as an arm of the executive, but also as a body directed by parliament to inquire and report, yet, by the will of that same parliament, to do so with "one arm tied behind its back". (RC 1.6.79)

The irony of this situation is that a parliament which has never been held in any significant regard by the wider community, which is frequently criticised in the media and in journal articles for its unprofessional performance, and which failed dismally in the *WA Inc* period to hold the executive accountable on a wide range of important matters, here refused an opportunity for the Royal Commission to examine important and relevant evidence concerning former and current members of an executive which had made some highly questionable decisions and had ridden roughshod over the parliament. Much of that evidence as requested by the

---

should be regarded as akin to arrest under the criminal law, so that no breach of privilege was involved.

Commission, in terms of the Hansard material, was already public and had been widely quoted and debated in the media in some instances.[6]

There is further irony in the fact that during most of the *WA Inc* period when State parliament was the centre of so much controversy, the State Governor was Gordon Reid, a former professor of politics and a former officer of the Commonwealth Parliament. Reid wrote extensively on the Commonwealth and State parliaments and relations between the "trinity of Crown [ie, the executive], Senate, and the House of Representatives . . . [where] the top prize in this trinitarian struggle is the Executive government and the power associated with its control". (Reid 1973, 515-16) Parliament's defence of its privileges using 300-year-old British precedent at the expense of the public interest would have fitted neatly into Reid's model. It was as if in the privilege issue parliament saw the Royal Commission as a competitor in the task of exposing political wrongdoing and was determined not to share the role any more than was necessary. It had already lost some ground, for while the Commission was sitting part of parliament's role had been relinquished in that parliamentary questions to ministers referring to the evidence of witnesses or other matters before the Royal Commission were inadmissible. (May 1989, 290) The incident also demonstrated that the State parliament, while legally free, even sovereign, remains firmly bound to the chariot wheels of British history – hardly the stuff of which either independent monarchies or republics are made.

In their final report the Commissioners' came back to this thorny question and to the original 300-year-old struggle between the Crown and parliament saying:

> The conviction which sustained the House of Commons during this struggle was that it was not fighting for its own privileges and benefit but in its representative capacity for the sake of the people as a whole.
>
> RC 1.6.70

They went on to link the existence of privilege directly with representative government and again quoted May (p 82) when he observed in the British context that:

> [T]he privilege which formerly protected members against action by the crown now serves largely as protection against their prosecution by individuals or corporate bodies. Consistently with this trend, sight may have

6 The failure to have privilege waived was not the only obstacle placed in the path of the Commission. It also failed to persuade the federal government to grant the same access to tax file information that was afforded to Queensland's Fitzgerald inquiry. (*Australian*, 22 October 1992)

> been lost of the original conception of the privilege as a protection devised in the interests of the public rather than for the protection of the individual member against the public. RC 1.6.71

Later, the Commissioners added:

> [I]n its origins, the privilege was asserted in its defence of the common people against the arbitrary power of the Executive. Its assertion in the present circumstances has been to inhibit the Commission in its search for the truth. (RC 6.78)

What made this whole episode quixotic was that, as mentioned at the start of this chapter, the opposition was quite able to mount a bill which sought to set aside executive privilege, cabinet secrecy or forms of legal privilege in order to establish a Royal Commission. Furthermore, in December 1993, when in government, the coalition announced that it was amending the former government's defence in the Bond Corporation's $960 million damages claim against the government in relation to the Petrochemicals Industries Company Ltd (PICL) agreement, the most notorious of all the *WA Inc* related references. The State argued that the 1988 agreement with Bondcorp was unenforceable because of unlawful and deceitful conduct involving public officials and members of the then government. This was because political donations amounting to millions of dollars given by Bond and others created a tendency for government ministers and public officers to use their power in a way that would favour the donors. (*West Australian*, 4 & 6 December 1993) The State Supreme Court, with damning Royal Commission findings to back its judgement agreed, it following from this that the State's obligations to its former partner were unenforceable.[7] It is of course ironic (but in no way improper) that while the Royal Commission was prevented from utilising parliamentary proceedings as part of its own inquiries, the executive successfully utilised the Commission's findings as part of a legal defence.

* * *

7 Obviously, this was a course of action which the former Labor government could not have contemplated but it quickly brought years of prospective and expensive legal argument to an end with a $7 million settlement and removed a major contingent liability from the State's balance sheet. (*West Australian*, 6 December 1993) Premier Court presaged that the government would look at taking action against certain parties to retrieve the money lost. The more notorious private sector players were bankrupt, in theory at least, but it was suggested that there were always former Labor ministers to pursue. However, when asked for his view former Premier Dowding raised a moot point, saying: "The whole of Cabinet made a series of decisions . . . those issues are raising very new views of responsibility". (*West Australian*, 7 December 1993)

But much of this was far in the future. To return to 1990, members of the Opposition parties were of course delighted with the setting up of the Commission, but this was less fòr the great principles of government involved than the political ammunition it would provide at the next election – obviously the same reason the government had not wanted the Commission created. Both the party caucuses and the non-parliamentary wings were equally as silent in anything that resembled serious constitutional discussion.

For all the attention which the Commissioners gave to the question of parliamentary privilege and how it would affect the quality of their inquiry, as well as to the meaning they would place on corrupt, illegal and improper behaviour, it is odd that they appeared to give no attention to the equally important concept of the public interest. This term was used widely in the Commission's report and had a key place in many of its more controversial findings. It would thus appear to require discussion not only for that reason but also because of its role in establishing the validity and applicability of the traditional public administration model, which the Commissioners' took largely for granted, as against its modern competitors and especially the public choice and collective choice models. (Lane 1993). Within the traditional model of public administration the idea of the public interest requires the existence of a special version of rationality, specifically, impartiality. Within this context bureaucrats would not only disregard their own irrational or non-rational interests but also their selfish interests. The peculiar standards this demands from bureaucrats is summed up in the well known statement by Walter Lippman (1955, 42):

> Living adults share, we must believe, the same public interest. For them, however, the public interest is mixed with, and is often at odds with, their private and special interests. Put this way, we can say, I suggest, that the public interest may be presumed to be what men would choose if they saw clearly, thought rationally, acted disinterestedly and benevolently.

Chapman (1988, 313) poses further problems:

> [H]ow much weight should be given to ruling groups or classes in society, how much knowledge of all the facts should be required before pronouncements are made, how should all the evidence be accumulated and interpreted, and what procedures should exist to ensure the balance between the public interest(s) being promoted and private interests being disturbed?

Within this context great numbers of public officials make numerous discretionary decisions every day where conceptions of the public interest are weighed against private interests. Such decisions are expected to apply the highest ethical standards but again, as Chapman, (1988, 298) notes:

> [I]n circumstances where there is, in theory, no limit to the care that might be taken, a balance has to be maintained between the rights and interests of individuals and groups, and the national (public) interest as indicated by the Crown and as interpreted by individual officials.

The Commissioners did not address these issues yet, as their report revealed, the public interest was frequently what some ministers and their advisers decided, unilaterally and unaccountably, it should be. Such behaviour was at times judged improper, but such judgements depend a great deal on the context and ethical stance one adopts towards the public interest, as will be explained in the next chapter.

A further weakness of the Commission was one common with many committees of inquiry, that is the monopoly of a single academic discipline, in this case law, among the investigators. Certainly other skills were called upon as required, these included accounting and information systems which were used extensively. It is difficult to establish from their report whether the Commission had a strategy in relation to the utilisation of an appropriate knowledge base for purposes of their inquiry and it may have been this narrow focus of expertise which produced several doubtful or mistaken judgements.

One possible error in their early procedures, for example, was not to place an immediate embargo on the destruction of select computer files in sensitive areas of government immediately upon their appointment. For example – but not exclusively – in the Ministry of Premier and Cabinet. The Commissioners intention should have been to declare it an offence to delete or in any way expunge material from the hard disc or from backup discs. The reason for suggesting this strategy relates to a recent case in the United States where the electronic mail system in the White House played a central role in the successful prosecution of Oliver North in the Iran-Contra scandal as the electronic messages North sent and received were used as primary evidence against him. North had attempted to delete these files when news of the scandal first broke but investigators were able to reconstruct them from back-up tapes of which North was unaware. As North told investigators later "We sincerely believed that when we . . . punched the delete button that it was gone forever. Wow, were we wrong" (*New Scientist*, 8 February 1992) Investigators were even able to retrieve some of North's deleted documents that were not recorded on backup tapes. There is no evidence that the Royal Commission considered this strategy or were advised of the option at any stage of their inquiries. Had they applied it in selected areas both the quantity and quality of evidence may have been greatly improved. In addition, the Commissioners made no recommendations on how the latest advances in computer technology may ensure a much improved integrity of the government's information systems. In modern fraudproof electronic record systems each document is allocated a "hash value/function", and, if anything is altered, the hash value will also be different and, if required, the identity of the "editor" can be established. (*New Scientist*, 29 February 1992) During their investigations the Commissioners expressed serious concern at the removal of yellow stickers from departmental files; on another occasion the local tip was being searched for dumped documents. However, while some private computers were sequestrated the contents of the unexplored electronic data banks of government computers held much more potential. This was illustrated when some former Petrochemicals Industries Company Ltd (PICL) (a major inquiry reference) computers were sold off there was some embarrassment as to the contents of their hard discs.[8]

A second weakness of the narrow knowledge base utilised by the Commission is illustrated by the mistaken interpretation placed on the term "whole of government" policy. This policy was brought in during the Burke years and was intended to bring about a better co-ordination and integration of government policy. This was partly accomplished by establishing a policy secretariat and a cabinet secretariat in the Department of Premier and Cabinet so as to break down the barriers to co-ordination – departmentalism – between government departments.

For example, when reporting on the government's most senior adviser, Kevin Edwards, the Commission wrote:

> It is also necessary to understand the attitude of Mr Burke to the role of statutory instrumentalities and, in particular, SGIC and GESB. We were told plainly by Mr Edwards and others, that SGIC and GESB were no more than arms of government which existed to fulfil the government's policy aims and objectives. Mr Burke said he regarded SGIC as a vehicle for investment by government. These views appeared to be the natural outcome of a "whole of government" approach to the practice of government which Mr Burke brought to his administration. . . . it was an approach adopted at serious cost to the State, not only in terms of money but also in terms of the integrity of the system of public administration.
>
> (RC 21.1.9)

The fact that the government regarded these statutory bodies as "hollow logs" and engaged in a measure of asset stripping is beyond

8 At the 1993-4 trial of Connell, the former managing director of Rothwells, a 1984 memo retrieved from an old computer was produced in evidence and played a vital role in bringing about a guilty verdict. My point here, however, is that government computer systems were not given the same attention.

doubt. However, to align this with "whole of government" strategy is to malign a policy that was well intended and necessary, even though it may not have been a roaring success.

A third weakness of this selective knowledge base was the narrow approach the Commission had to acquiring evidence. Its approach was simply to talk with anyone who was close to the action, to interrogate, to examine financial and other records, to piece together available data in following money trails; in other words, to use what was available. There was of course a general invitation issued to anyone to volunteer information to the Commission if they wished, and no doubt some did. Equally however, others would certainly have been intimidated and wary about making their views known.

While it would not have been useful as evidence in a court of law, to survey a sample of public service opinion, asking questions about specific matters related to the references would have possibly endorsed some of the findings the Commissioners reached by other means – always a useful research strategy. Indeed, while the Commission was sitting such a survey was undertaken by Curtin University on the ethical standards current in the Senior Executive Service at that time. The resulting analysis serves as a basis for Chapter 5. However, there was room for several more surveys to serve both as a check on the conclusions reached by the Commissioners and to serve as a benchmark against which later improvements may be measured. In this case a great opportunity was missed.

Despite these suggested weaknesses in the Commission's approach, each of which had the potential to change the nature of the outcome, the overall quality of the report provided a major insight into the more murky areas of government dealings in Western Australia during the 1980s.

References

Black D (ed) (1991). *The House on the Hill: A History of the Parliament of Western Australia 1832-1990*, Perth, Parliament of Western Australia.

Chapman, RA (1988). *Ethics in the British Civil Service*, London, Routledge.

Lane J-E (1993). *The Public Sector: Concepts, Models and Approaches*, London, Sage.

Lippman W (1955). *Essays in the Public Interest Philosophy*, Boston, Little Brown.

Marshall G in Vernon Bogdanor (1987). *The Blackwell Encyclopaedia of Political Institutions*, Oxford, Blackwell.

May, Erskine (1989). *Parliamentary Practice*, 21st ed, London, Butterworths.

Okely B and Black D. *Parliamentary Privilege in Western Australia* in Black op cit, 385-428.

Reid GS and Forrest M (1989). *Australia's Commonwealth Parliament 1901-1988: Ten Perspectives*, Melbourne UP.

Reid GS (1973). "The Trinitarian Struggle: Parliamentary-Executive Relationships" in Mayer H and Nelson H (eds), *Australian Politics: A Third Reader*, Melbourne, Cheshire, 513-26.

4

WA Inc:

Failure of the System or Crime of the Employee?

Allan Peachment

The legacy[1]

The abbreviation *Inc*, for *Incorporated*, proved to be a handy label to tag onto select states in Australia during the eighties. It allowed politicians and others to get across a complicated message in very simple terms, even though the meaning differed from one state to another. For example, in New South Wales the term *NSW Inc* was a shorthand expression for a market forces oriented government; but in Western Australia *WA Inc* referred to that series of financial disasters and political scandals which swept through the state in the late 1980s. The resulting debt is estimated at between $1 and $1.5 billion. (Peachment 1991, 188-91; Harman 1990, 25) But the legacy of *WA Inc* was not restricted to financial losses brought on by business-government deals which failed or the bailout of financial institutions which were incompetently managed; there were other instances of failure which might count for more in the longer term. For example, state parliament, which in representative terms was never a progressive institution, was debauched, with accountability of the executive to parliament being almost non-existent; the senior public service, while being improved in some regards, was crudely and selectively politicised in others – the mid-ranks of the service being confused and demoralised in the process; in the early years especially the Perth and inter-state media was hypnotised by the former journalist

1 References to RC indicate Royal Commission, followed by the number of the appropriate paragraph in the report.

Premier and rather than enhancing accountability in its role as the fourth estate became the unwitting captive of government; local entrepreneurs, among the nation's most successful and admired, if not infamous, became major financial backers of their old foe, the Australian Labor Party – or more accurately, its leader, Brian Burke. Finally, academia which provided a pool of talent at that time, most of whom went to the federal sphere, was tempted to make a further contribution in state government, a move which reduced the already small number of conflict of interest free commentators.

The English translation of *pantonflage*, parachuting – a well known expression in French government – became a household word to describe the placement of senior officers, principal private secretaries with an empathy – sometimes much more – for Labor policies, into strategic positions in many parts of the wider bureaucracy.[2] According to survey evidence many of these appointments were regarded as having a serious and negative effect on the ethical standards of the service. (see Chapter 5) Consultants were often an excessively expensive engine for managerialist private sector style reform. Nor was their recruitment restricted to local, national and international talent, but included the Premier (O'Connor) who had lost the previous election! O'Connor, his successor, Burke, and Deputy-Premier Parker, two senior advisers, Edwards and Lloyd, were later to face criminal charges and four other senior public servants were charged under the *Public Service Act* having been found to have acted improperly. (*West Australian*, 10 November 1992)

Elements of the private sector were no less deeply involved in many of the key disasters, indeed, almost all of the state's prominent entrepreneurs were major players – and losers. It was no comfort to observe that the governments of Victoria and South Australia underwent financial collapse of a more significant magnitude, as earlier chapters have described. Nevertheless, it is worth noting that in the more global version of *WA Inc* that was played out in a number of countries, speculation, greed and incredibly irresponsible and unethical practice resulted in huge government and private losses culminating in the October 1987 – and later – stockmarket collapse. Following the 1987 crash, in 1990 the Nikkei Dow index declined 49% from 38,915 on the last trading day of 1989 to 19,782 on 1 October, a deeper drop than Wall Street suffered in the 1929 crash. (Taylor 1993; Rees-Mogg & Davidson 1989, 18; Lawson 1992, [Ch 32 *Fraud and the City*]).

---

2 Ian Radbone notes that this was a minor phenomenon in South Australia during the Bannon years.

WA Inc: A failure of the system?

Returning to the question posed by the chapter title it is clear that if what occurred during the *WA Inc* saga was a result of a failure of the system, then the system, so called, is a highly variegated phenomenon. It is, in this case, a vast interlocking directorate which includes all the organisations listed above; parliament, public bureaucracies, the media, high-flying entrepreneurs, consultants and select individuals in academia and the private sector. It must also include relationships between political parties, their leaders and their elected nominees in parliament, especially ministers; between ministers and their key advisers and between key advisers themselves. To place the label "corporatism" on this without relating to established theory, as some have done, is to oversimplify a distinctive episode in Western Australian history. (O'Brien 1986, 1991; Peachment 1992)

That "the system" failed is not seriously in doubt. As already mentioned (see Chapter 3), while offering to waive some aspects of privilege, the system failed when party leaders and others refused to conditionally waive parliamentary privilege in order to assist the investigations of the Royal Commission. Indeed, by making certain statements unexaminable, this action may have crippled the Commission at a stroke. On the other hand, while the practice of public administration in Western Australia has many shortcomings, the Royal Commission misjudged the situation when it asserted that:

> Public administration in the late twentieth century in this State is being conducted under what, in essence, is a late nineteenth century legislative framework.
>
> (RC 6.2.1)

If this was the case in the 1980s then it was more the case in earlier decades and for this reason could hardly be counted as a cause of *WA Inc*.

This sweeping and complicated canvas tends to baffle rather than assist in understanding *WA Inc*. Attempts to draw the linkages and connections between the various players tend to look more like the wiring diagram for an ICBM missile than anything else. The most successful attempt to come to grips with this challenge has been that of Elizabeth

Harman. (1990)[3] Harman's paper sets out two main arguments in her attempt to assist in coming to grips with events of the 1980s. Nominating accountability as one of the main problems she argues that *WA Inc:*

> [C]an only be understood in the context of the historical political struggle for power between Labor and non-Labor parties . . . (this in turn is related to) the struggle between the Executive and Parliament; – or, more accurately, between the Executive and the Conservative dominated upper house.

Apart from describing the threats by the Council to block supply Harman does not explore this theme further but concentrates instead on her second argument which states that *WA Inc* was not a single phenomenon but several quite distinct phases in the relationship between government and business. Thus the motives, key actors, actions and outcomes differ in each phase.

Harman's six suggested phases are not mutually exclusive and are only roughly chronological. The first phase was the Burke government's creation of new government-business enterprises (GBE's) between 1983-84 so as to take the Labor government strongly into commercial activities following its election win. These new creations included (a) the acquisition of a company which in turn led to the creation of over 20 subsidiaries and, (b) the establishment of new statutory corporations with wide investment powers. The second phase was the realignment of the old GBEs which included the Government Employees Superannuation Board and the government insurance arms which later became the SGIC. These older GBE's controlled substantial investment funds and, as in other states, their control by government was part of the search for "hollow logs". Two additional GBEs which were part of this were the Rural and Industries Bank and the State Energy Commission. Harman's term "realignment" is a euphemism for something much more sinister; however, her further comment that these changes went largely unnoticed at the time and that the media focused on the wrong targets, throws a powerful light on important developments.

Harman refers to her third phase as "The Partisan Element" which was concerned with the establishment of overt links between big business and the ALP and in particular with the establishment of the John Curtin

3 I thank Elizabeth Harman for permission to quote extensively from her unpublished paper.

fundraising foundation.[4] The fourth phase was Rights and Property Deals which concerned the involvement of government and mainly prominent entrepreneurs in a range of deals relating to older public sector sites. The potential and the reality for indulging in "scams" and doing deals with mates was considerable. The fifth phase was the rescue from failure of local financial institutions from 1987 onwards. The sums required to save some of these bodies from liquidation included $16.7 million for the Swan Building Society and $129.6 million for the Teachers Credit Society. It also included the first of three rescues of Rothwells merchant bank at the cost of $370 million. Within each of these financial institutions "'incredible irresponsible and unethical banking practice" was uncovered – the old safeguards failed dismally. Harman's final, most complicated and expensive phase occurred in 1988 and involved the government purchase of a share in the Petroleum Industries Corporation Limited (PICL) and the second and third attempted rescues of Rothwells. Briefly, Harman argues that the second rescue was a scam to allow corporate players to recover funds and did not assist in Rothwells liquidity crisis. Realising the highly adverse publicity that would result at a third Rothwells rescue the government, with the connivance of private interests, dressed it up as an investment which was attractive to the long-term development of the State. The Bill to allow the deal was rejected by the Legislative Council and it collapsed.

Harman's six phases no doubt help clarify this complicated situation and she goes on to extract further points from her analysis which are also useful. However, there are other circumstances which should be mentioned as part of a wider analysis. For example, while Harman correctly notes the importance of the historical power struggle between Labor and non-Labor with its focus on the Council, of equal importance is the State government's attempts, as with all State governments, to maximise its independence from reliance of inter-governmental financial transfers and the conditions attached to these. (Peachment 1991, 191-92; Schapper 1993) Thus to raise revenue from sources other than the Commonwealth or the State parliament was doubtless a critical part of the strategy. Indeed, had they worked as the government hoped they would, all but the fifth phase, have had the potential for adding to the government's revenue base. Even phase five, had it have worked, would have helped retain some of the State's existing financial base in working order. Of

---

4 Western Australian entrepreneurs and businessmen gave more than $6 million to the Australian Labor Party during the 1980s, much of it through the Curtin Foundation. (*West Australian* 23 May 1992)

course, none of this is to in any way accept the inexcusably bad management and unethical and improper behaviour which was associated with these developments and which was uncovered by both the McCusker[5] inquiry into Rothwells and the Royal Commission.

A major weakness with the Harman categorisation scheme however, is that while it purports to deal with the relationship between government and business some important ingredients are missing. For example, it is arguable that both running through and affecting each of the six phases are two themes each of which had a major impact on *WA Inc*. First, there is the role of the media which in the modern world is a potent component of accountability – a concept to which Harman's paper gives considerable attention. Kennedy (1991) has written much on how some members of the press in particular were seduced by Brian Burke in particular and how this helped "manage" the news. Burke was extraordinarily accessible to the media and enjoyed strong rapport with both journalists and media executives. Interviews became sounding boards for policy initiatives and his way of handling his media critics was to "love them to death" by seeking their opinions on issues. Burke's influence with the media effectively gave the impression of involving it in formulating the policy agenda – a heady brew. This in turn must have reduced its role and impact in reporting issues to do with accountability – it tended to report the parliamentary circus not the political circumstances.

Much the same can be claimed for the second theme – that of ministerial advisers. There is now available significant primary survey evidence which is strongly suggests that the major infusion of ministerial advisers which took place from day one of the Burke regime did major damage far beyond their relatively slight numbers. While advisers of a kind were not new to government and while some of those appointed made a solid and positive contribution – as a body, the evidence against them and their negative ethical impact on public sector processes and outcomes is overwhelming. (See Chapter 5) These two themes of the media and ministerial advisers would each have impacted on all six of Harman's categories as well as on the additional category of federal-State financial relations. The overall result of this was that the existing system, distorted by an unrepresentative upper chamber and massive fiscal imbalance in the

5 The *Report of Inspector on a Special Investigation into Rothwells Ltd* (McCusker) was set up on 8 March 1989 to examine the affairs of Rothwells during the period 1 January 1985 to 31 December 1988. The 381-page report (Part 1) was released on 29 August 1990.

federal system together made the role of a State Labor government more difficult than that of a coalition government to fulfil was, perhaps initially, counterbalancing but eventually was further distorted by the factors described above.

Having set down some of the difficulties in comprehending the wider ramifications of *WA Inc,* in particular in how they may relate to it being a failure of the system, this part of the analysis will continue by examining the various remedies put forward by those who debated the circumstances at the time.

In response to the Part II report of the Royal Commission, commentators have proposed a wide-ranging and diverse series of reforms. These may be placed in one of two alternative categories the first of which proposes entirely new arrangements for the structure and processes of government and the second, following the lead given by the Royal Commission, advocates a transformation and upgrading of existing political institutions and processes. There is a degree of overlap between these two positions.

The first group[6] notes the problems which stem from the "demonstrated inadequacies" in certain of WA's constitutional provisions and practices whereby "any party in power will attempt to use its authority to the limit simply because the powers are there". (O'Brien & Webb 1991, 12) The so-called *Executive State* which results from these inadequacies is claimed to obviate those gains attained through England's *Magna Carta* and Glorious Revolution and which were part of WA's constitutional heritage. The authors' reform strategy is to propose a new State constitution which entrenches limitations on government, and specifies State "sovereignty" – a term the meaning of which the group appears to regard as self-evident – a declaration of rights, a separation of powers beyond that which already exists, even a new State animal emblem, the banded anteater. (O'Brien & Webb, 346) Because of their wide ranging and radical nature the reform proposals this group may be described as "maximalist".

In addition, this group also seeks to promote the idea of "executive recall", an idea which, to the ideological discomfort of its promoters, was first mooted by Karl Marx. (Bogdanor 1987, 522) This suggested reform would give the electorate the potential power to remove any elected or appointed official whether in parliament, the public service or the

---

6 This group is composed of Professors Patrick O'Brien and Martyn Webb (University of Western Australia), the pressure group, People for Fair and Open Government, and the private think tank, the Institute of Public Affairs.

judiciary. In effect it would largely replace the parliamentary vote of no-confidence and thus lessen the influence of parties in the parliamentary system. On the other hand, as overseas experience has demonstrated, it may also be used to intimidate members of the judiciary as well as other senior holders of public office who may make unpopular decisions. A similar suggestion of this group, the citizen-initiated referendum (CIR), was proposed as a means of allowing electors, under certain conditions, to both repeal Acts of Parliament or to make new laws without parliamentary intervention. This idea, as with others of their programme, was used with varying degrees of success by the "New Right" in the United States two decades ago.

The "maximalists" disregard the unimposing historical record of these proposed reforms. For example, in both the United States and Switzerland, the majority of initiative proposals not endorsed by the legislature have been rejected by the electorate. The CIR also increases the influence of interest groups in given policy outcomes, as well as the influence of those with resources and in this sense has little to do with "citizens" or with educating the wider public.

What is equally as contradictory is that the "maximalist" group includes individuals who have consistently called for smaller, and thus cheaper, and less intrusive government, but have ignored the cost to the taxpayer of frequent referenda. Nor, apparently, have they considered the question of the politicisation of the electorate that would result from frequent calls to debate complex political matters and vote in referenda.

In their reform proposals, the second of the two groups,[7] which may be termed "political pragmatists", take greater account of what is politically achievable. Their aim is to see Western Australia's version of the Westminster system reformed rather than replaced, thus, they begin with the recommendations of the Royal Commission and urge the setting up of independent parliamentary agencies to oversee reform and renewal in all its dimensions. Their list of reform proposals does not differ greatly from mooted proposals in other troubled political systems, although generally, the Western Australian versions are less developed. (Garrett 1992; Brazier 1991; Hailsham 1992; Mount 1992; Lenman 1992) They include strengthening both individual and collective ministerial responsibility, improving the potential of parliamentary committees to "heckle the steam-roller" and reviewing alternative voting systems. To the

7 This group is made up of Professors Peter Boyce and Hugh Collins (Murdoch University.

extent that the origins of *WA Inc* lie in a failure of the system, this group realistically addresses that specific problem.

While the views of this second group are worthy of serious consideration this is not to say that little reform had taken place under Labor. Indeed, in less than a decade, in response to Commonwealth financial pressures, interstate and overseas example as well as far sighted ministers and some senior public servants (both before and after the election of Burke) the politician-managers of the day instituted some progressive public sector change. Much of this was aimed at making government departments run more efficiently and effectively and, while it caused much cynicism and loss of morale among the lower ranks, it did seem to be a step in the right direction. The process speeded up under Labor with the creation of policy and cabinet secretariats which sought to reduce the disadvantages of departmentalism and bring about "whole of government policy"; there was also an improved impetus given to departmental accountability through both the *Financial Administration and Audit Act* and the undertaking of functional reviews – this latter initiative perhaps even leading the Thatcher government's famous "scrutinies". How well the move succeeded is hard to say as there was little in the way of evaluation. Survey evidence suggests that the parachuting in of a cadre of ministerial advisers, as mentioned above, was probably the most controversial move of all; their mixed talents were in one sense the jewel in Labor's crown, in another sense, an ethical sense, they were one of Labor's pall-bearers. Dickens' words: "It was the best of times . . . the worst of times . . . the age of wisdom . . . the age of foolishness . . . the epoch of belief . . . the epoch of incredulity . . . we had everything before us. . .", sum up the difficulties of discerning the most accurate interpretation of all these events.

WA Inc: Crime of the employee?

If *WA Inc* resulted from a "crime of the employee" set of factors in the sense that select employees of the State, particularly ministers, advisers and senior public servants, were aware of the occurrence of corrupt, illegal or improper behaviour, then a different set of questions are raised which address cultural attitudes and ethical standards in the public sector. For example: what do such individuals understand by the term ethics? What factors most influence their personal ethical standards? How often have they experienced ethical dilemmas in the workplace? What is their formal response to such dilemmas? How do they feel about "whistle blowing"? Are they aware of, and how do they relate to official guidelines in this area? To what extent do they believe there is a significant ethical problem in the public sector and which organisations or individuals do they believe should exercise leadership in this regard? For example, their own agency, a central agency, parliament, politicians or professional bodies? Finally, what do they believe to be the impact of those powerful new recruits, ministerial advisers on the ethical standards of the public sector? Recent research into the State's public and the private sector now allow appropriate judgements to be made on these questions which, together with their accompanying arguments, will be presented in Chapter 5.

However, before considering that evidence, and in line with the preceding discussion of the broad principles and developments surrounding *WA Inc* as a failure of "the system", what follows is a comparable discussion on *WA Inc* as a "crime of the employee".

Figure 4.1 sets down a suggested analytical framework for dealing with this aspect of the question. Essentially, this matrix allows for the consideration of the two concepts of "crime" and "employee". The heading crime is intended to denote the illegal, improper or corrupt outcome of a policy, one which has come about as a result of behaviour which may be classified in ethical terms as either deontological or teleological. These and other terms require explanation.

Figure 4.1: Framework for Analysing the Concepts Crime and Employee

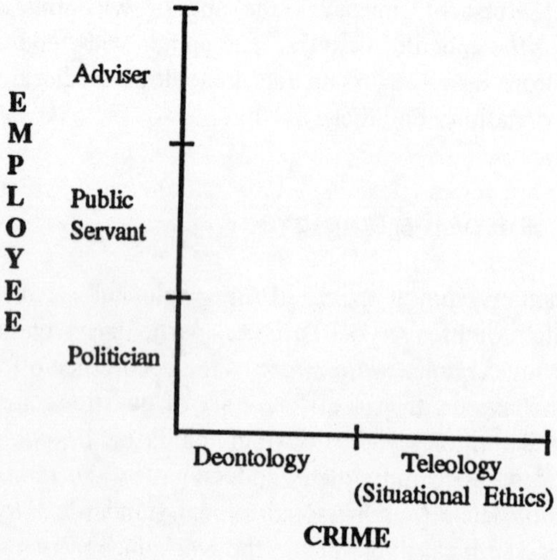

Deontology

Deontology involves behaviour which focuses on the notion of duty where each component of a decision is judged on its merits in terms of rules, standards and codes of conduct. Problems may arise from the use of deception, bribery and other morally objectionable means as there is an expectation in these circumstances that the rules and procedures developed and applied by government officials will be in harmony with more idealistic and commonly held values. Those who carry out orders blindly and seek to excuse themselves from responsibility for unethical actions with explanations such as "I was just following orders"; "If I didn't do it, someone else would have"; "I had no choice", may be guilty of a crime even if a duty statement specifies that orders from a superior must be obeyed. Some writers (Rosen 1989, 164-65) Cahill and Overman (1988, 17, 41) note Rohr's distinction in this regard between a "low road" approach which addresses ethical issues almost exclusively in terms of "adherence to agency rules" regardless of the consequences, and a "high road" approach associated with the "new" public administration where social equity and justice may be added to the classical norms of efficient, economic and co-ordinated management.

Teleology or situational ethics

Teleological decision-making behaviour, on the other hand, is that which considers the end result or outcome of a policy to be paramount and to override the means by which it has been attained. This is the "end justifies the means" approach, or to describe it in more modern jargon "situational ethics". Public policies and governmental actions are replete with examples that are teleological in nature. Circumstances that may justify one set of policies at one point in time may prove them morally reprehensible at a later date.

For example, in the 1930s, Sir Christopher Bullock, then Permanent Secretary to the Air Ministry in Britain, was one of a number of senior officials who, unauthorised, continually supplied Winston Churchill with classified government information, in this case figures of German air strength. (Griffith & Ryle 1989, 30) Churchill, who was then a backbencher, used this information to effectively criticise and embarrass the government of the day and to alert the people of Britain to the potential threat from the Luftwaffe. None of these officials was criticised for their unauthorised actions, done in the "public interest", and Churchill was later to become Prime Minister. Bullock was dismissed from the British civil service in 1936 for reasons unconnected with the above incident; it was perhaps that he was too entrepreneurial for his own good. (Chapman 1988, 303)

Two decades later, in 1956, it was alleged that Sir Norman Brook, then Head of the British Civil Service, communicated the Eden government's confidential plans for the Suez venture – of which he disapproved – to the Americans through the intelligence network. The subsequent lack of American support for the venture was instrumental in bringing about a humiliating Anglo- French climb-down. Sir Norman was later made a peer of the realm. Again, in 1984, Sir Frank Cooper, former Secretary of State for the Ministry of Defence, said on television that the leaking of information by service chiefs, worried about the consequences of government defence reviews, could be justified.

These above examples of British officials leaking information in an effort to strengthen opposition to government policy in a bid to safeguard what they each regarded as the "national interest" may be contrasted with an American example, one of many, which today military officers describe as "situational ethics". This view of ethics argues that a higher end, such as national security, justifies lying and deception in public affairs. The examples in question concern the so-called Iran-Contra affair where US administration officials arranged to sell arms secretly to the government of Iran, with some of the proceeds then being used to provide funds for the rebels (the Contras) fighting against the government of Nicaragua. Diversion of the funds violated the Boland Amendment which prohibited assistance from the US government to the Contras during several periods in the 1980s. Appearing before the Senate's Iran-Contra inquiry Admiral Poindexter did not offer a denial when he was accused of holding an "unapologetic embrace of untruth". Instead he justified his position by saying "I think that the actions that I took were in the long term interests of the country". Poindexter's view was supported by then Secretary of Defence, Caspar Weinberger who, at the same inquiry said, "I don't see how you can leave aside situational or other ethics" (Richter 1990, 130-131)

In each of the above cases senior government employees breached convention or formal guidelines, taking it upon themselves, for allegedly the President had no knowledge of this, to behave in an unauthorised and possibly illegal or improper manner so as to promote what they believed was the more appropriate policy. In each case they promoted policy contrary to the publicly-espoused policy of legitimately-elected governments.

What these examples have in common is that many upright citizens would have agreed with the actions taken. Indeed, in the Winston Churchill example, it is difficult to imagine anyone claiming Bullock was anything but a hero. However, in the Australian context, Sir Arthur Tange, former secretary of the Department of Defence, has said:

> I see no advantage to the nation's good government in adding support to a right in individual servants to make their own rules, . . . Similarly, I would characterize and condemn unauthorised disclosure of documents not simply as larrikin activity . . . but as self-serving. If there is said in justification in some cases that conscience requires accountability to a higher duty, that to my mind adds arrogance to the breach of professional duty.
>
> Tange 1981, 5

Apart from wondering what course world history may have taken had Bullock followed this advice, it would seem that judging the "effectiveness" of an official action by the motives that drive it is not a reliable guide to deciding right from wrong; if indeed, there can be such a distinction in ethical affairs. As one ethics scholar has written:

> I would be perfectly content to get people to perform good acts and abstain from bad ones for whatever motives we can. Doing the right thing for the wrong reason is fine by me – or, anyway, I do not think that doing it for the wrong reason in anyway undermines the rightness of the action.
>
> Goodin, 8

It may be that some governments already adopt this philosophy which is why no recorded action was taken against the British officials cited above. In the American example, which focused on the trial of former marine colonel, Oliver North, the court's finding of guilty was later reversed by the US Court of Appeals. (North 1991, 412)

This then is the difficulty. How, and at what point in time, should such actions be judged and what principles of public administration, can serve as a guide? For example, the manner in which British officials for years helped organise the breaching of their own government's official oil embargo against Rhodesia was clearly illegal, yet no action was taken against them. There are no doubt many Australian equivalents. (Wilenski 1979, 44; Grabosky 1989)

The situation becomes even more frustrating when ethical dilemmas arise from implicit knowledge, such as when elected representatives cannot and will not act in relation to the resolution of a given problem but who make their inner thoughts known informally to advisers who, without further communication, determine to act without authority in a manner they believe their leader prefers. The remark "Who will rid me of this turbulent priest?" and the subsequent fate of Thomas a Beckett is a good illustration of one possible outcome which raises serious concerns for democratically-elected governments. It is not of course a new phenomenon. (Haynes 1992)

Reverting to the Western Australian context the issue is in some instances more clear cut. The Royal Commission's report, commenting on "impropriety of considerable proportions" stated "our abiding concern is that many elected and appointed officials appeared to have little understanding of their role and responsibility and of the standards of conduct to be expected of them". (RC 27.2.10) More specifically the Commission noted that:

> Members of statutory authorities with very significant public funds subject to their control, have seemed to be unaware of, or at least indifferent to, their legal and public duties.
>
> (RC 27.2.4)

Reflecting on the above ethical dilemmas, the extent to which *WA Inc* may be regarded as a "crime" of the employee resulting from behaviour of the kind described above, requires, among other things, clarification of the term "employee". The vertical axis "Employee" of Fig 4.1 contains three sub-headings: "politician", "public servant" and "adviser" which are intended to represent the full scope of the concept "Employee" in public sector terms. Fig 4.1 thus provides six categories each of which is discussed below and is analysed utilising empirical evidence and findings taken from the report of the Royal Commission. Chapter 5 which deals with survey evidence of the views of senior public servants and ministerial advisers is used to corroborate or falsify the results.

Politicians

New members of the parliament are drawn from almost every conceivable background and frequently demonstrate inadequacies in their elected position. On their lack of understanding of the procedures of the parliament, the legislative process and ethics, former Premier Carmen Lawrence, a trained psychologist with an interest in parliamentary behaviour, has said:

> These are things you have to determine on the job and the difficulty is that you can make some pretty appalling mistakes and those mistakes can be the subject of considerable public criticism.
>
> Quoted in McMahon (1991, 130)

If this is the general situation among newly elected or inexperienced backbenchers then, during the Burke-Dowding years of office the Commissioners' view was that inappropriate behaviour was of much more serious concern among even senior ministers. Of former Premier Burke they concluded that, in relation to various references, the "concessions" he made under cross-examination were "quite unconvincing"; that he was "not prepared to be candid and open with the police or the Commission". There were several references to Mr Burke acting "improperly" or engaging in "improper conduct", and of his conduct being "seriously deficient". In summary, the Commissioners found that Mr Burke "acted improperly, his conduct being discreditable and amounting to a substantial breach of the standard of rectitude to be expected of a person holding the office of Premier". [General references] (RC 10.7.17), (RC 10.18.9), (RC 10.18.15), (RC 10.19.31), (RC 10.33.4), (RC 10.33.12), (RC 21.1.12), (RC 21.1.17), (RC 21.1.26), (RC 24.11.16), (RC 24.11.26), (RC 24.11.29). Mr Burke did not comment publicly on these findings.

In the case of former Deputy Premier David Parker the Commission's findings were, if anything, more serious. Of Parker the Commission said that he was:

> [A]rticulate and highly intelligent with a very quick mind. . . . extremely confident to the point of arrogance. . . . (that he had) made insufficient concessions to the limited experience which he had accumulated up to the time when he became the Minister for SECWA.

It went on to say that his evidence was "evasive and quite lacking in conviction", that he himself was "totally unconvincing", that he was "grossly negligent", that "by any normal measure of the conduct of a Minister of the Crown, his behaviour was grossly incompetent, if not absurd. That the conduct would have been improper goes without saying". As with Burke, the Commission found Parker's behaviour was "completely irresponsible and fell far short of the standard of rectitude expected and required of a Minister". [General references] (RC 10.5.10), (RC 10.7.18), (RC 10.9.9), (RC 10.23.23), (RC 10.23.26), (RC 10.27.7), (RC 10.27.10), (RC 10.27.16), (RC 10.29.11), (RC 10.29.30), (RC 10.31.8), (RC 10.33.2), (RC 10.33.4), (RC 10.33.14).

The Commission found that Parker's role in the SECWA/Bondcorp deal to be an example of "improper action" and that "If Mr Parker paused to consider the wider interests of the public, which must have been clearly evident to him, he did not pause for long". (RC 21.1.131) In relation to Parker's statement that "government world-wide is built on the basis of concealment" the Commissioners judged that:

> This reveals a profound misconception of the proper role of Government. It is a misconception which, unfortunately, seems to have been commonplace amongst some of his government colleagues, in particular, the Premier, Mr Dowding.
>
> (RC 21.1.11)

Unfortunately the misconception here may, more likely, be that of the Commissioners, as some of the examples of the deliberate breaching of national security policy for a personal view of the national good, given above, suggest.

The third major witness upon whom the Commissioners commented was former Premier, Peter Dowding. On one reference the Commissioners found his evidence to be "full of circularity designed to evade the obvious conclusion" and that he prevaricated. They also found that he had "not been frank" and in another respect that his evidence was "unconvincing". In another instance the Commissioners refused to accept his evidence, while in relation to Rothwells one of his decisions "was one of the high points in a sustained course of improper conduct involving himself, Mr Parker and Mr Grill". Similarly, in relation to the PICL deal it was found that the total course of conduct which these three ministers engaged in was "grossly improper". [General references] (RC 19.8.10), (RC 19.8.13), (RC 19.9.17), (RC 19.9.34), (RC 20.1.5), (RC 20.3.10), (RC 21.1.56), (RC 21.1.111), (RC 21.1.121), (RC 21.1.129), (RC 21.1.151).

Mr Dowding was one of those who disputed the Commission's findings. He admitted that he had deliberately concealed details from the public, saying he had done so to protect the government's commercial interests. But he took exception to the Commission's finding that he had mislead cabinet over major developments, saying he had told members everything he knew at that time, adding:

> It's convenient, perhaps, to some people still in office to try to suggest that, at that time, what they were informed of was different from my state of knowledge.
>
> *West Australian* 22 October 1992

Dowding blamed his government's lack of business and financial expertise for the problems of *WA Inc* adding that he had been advised by several people who had not had the expertise to give such advice.[8] Dowding's views on his advisers is critical for what is to be analysed in later chapters particularly as he added that some of the advisers had left while others had become powerful in Western Australia and were advising Premier Lawrence. (*Australian* 22 October 1992)

In expressing his disappointment with the Commissioners' judgements which, he said, were "utterly wrong" in many cases he asserted that they had a "breathtakingly naive lack of understanding of the pressure and workload of political office". Touching on the ethics of his government's term of office he said that the Commissioners' "perception of what was right and proper might differ violently from the government's perception at that time".

Another former Premier, Ray O'Connor, said that he was surprised by the Commissions findings that he had deliberately leaked information about the Liberal Party to Premier Burke and that he had acted as a bagman for Bond Corporation to deliver a $25,000 bribe which he allegedly kept for himself. (*Australian* 22 October 1992) O'Connor is yet to stand trial.

In an outstanding example of ministerial responsibility in action the only minister to immediately resign on the tabling of the Commission's report was environment minister Bob Pearce. Pearce, while rejecting the Commission's findings, said that Westminster conventions compelled him to resign when he had been found to have acted improperly by using confidential financial records, supplied by suspended Financial Institutions Registrar John Metaxas, to discredit the Opposition during a 1987 parliamentary debate. He said he would not contest the next election.

Perhaps the most spectacular objections to the Royal Commission's findings came from Labor minister Julian Grill who rejected the finding that he had acted grossly improperly throughout his involvement in the disastrous petrochemical project. Grill asserted on television that the Commission had not acted independently or in all cases honestly. (*Australian* 22 October 1992; *West Australia* 22 October 1992) A collage of his later remarks would read as follows – the Commission had been influenced by the press, that it had been a media circus for quite some time and it continues to be one; that some of the findings are not supported by the evidence in any sense at all; that the Commission was judge, jury and

8 The most senior adviser, Kevin Edwards, suggested to the Commission that Dowding was an actor who could not distinguish between reality and illusion. Dowding responded that he was deceived by Edwards who was once a trusted employee. (*West Australian*, 11 April 1992)

executioner and people should be allowed to have independent positions as to its findings. Grill's position was endorsed by neither the Premier nor the party but he continued to pursue it publicly at appropriate intervals in later years.[9]

That the Commissioners findings may not have been beyond reproach gains some credence from the only other resignation to occur, that of Cabinet Secretary Bill Thomas. Thomas was found to have interfered with Cabinet records from a period before he entered parliament but insisted that his actions were well meant and intended as a response to criticism in the Commission on deficiencies in the official cabinet record. So confident was he of his position that he wrote to the Commission and reported his actions. The Commissioners decided that Thomas's actions belatedly tried to record the decision, evidence of which had been located in the Department of Premier and Cabinet, to seek submissions for the casino project, but had done so inaccurately. How so was not explained. How this could be interpreted as offending established mechanisms for accountability as well as the establishment of an accurate historical record of government is puzzling.

Public servants

The second category of employee to be examined in Fig 4.1 is that of public servants. While it was suggested earlier that ministers may have limited knowledge of governmental procedures and processes, their knowledge of the professional and constitutional relationship between themselves and their senior advisers often leaves just as much to be desired. As a starting point, what Chapman has written on the relationship between the British civil servant and policy has wide application here in Australia:

> [C]ivil servants play a uniquely important role in the constitution. They offer advice on constitutional practice, they interpret the constitutional conventions and sometimes write them down for the guidance of others, they produce detailed rules and administrative procedures that may affect and influence the way government works on a day to day basis, and by the development and maintenance of departmental policies they ensure continuity in government and have a vital role to play in the balance between policy and administration. . . . it is in these circumstances the role of civil servants becomes crucial. How they should behave when they are carrying out instructions of ministers, when they are acting on behalf of ministers, and when they are making policy proposals and advising ministers is not written

9 On 12 January 1995, after a four-year investigation by the Royal Commission investigation unit, Mr Grill was charged with stealing $20,000 from the ALP Eyre electorate campaign fund in 1989.

> down in the British system of government. Indeed, no comprehensive statement along these lines can be produced without fundamental changes in the constitution.
>
> Chapman 1988, 290-91

The more committed political role of senior public servants has been widely written about in both Britain and Australia and is well known, as are the terms used to describe them – "statesmen in disguise" and "cloistered politicians", roles acted out on television in *Yes Minister.* Indeed, several ministers, both State and federal, have made reference to *Yes Minister* in public statements to illustrate their views on senior members of their departments. Other senior ministers have given detailed examples of how their advisers sought to blatantly manipulate and control them, often with considerable success. (Hayden 1980, 425-28; Sinclair 1976, 5). Alternatively, the convention that ministers can be relied upon to defend the decisions of their public servants in parliament or in the media can no longer be taken for granted. Obviously, any idea of there being an reciprocity of duty between ministers and advisers which reflects a deontological relationship has, to some extent, been set aside. This makes calls for an upgrading of ministerial responsibility a very doubtful strategy, although not in Western Australia at this present time given the doctrine's new lease of life.

For those public servants who continue to serve their minister with a sense of duty, that is the great majority, these developments have been confusing and frustrating. Some ministers are now less accessible to their senior officials since the advent of principle private secretaries and ministerial advisers and serve the minister at a distance. Indeed, when senior officials in Western Australia were asked whom or what did they regard themselves as serving in their daily work situation, and were given five options (the Minister, the government, the Crown, the parliament, the public) the response was highly differentiated. (Chapter 5) In terms of the constitutional position on this question, while the public servant serves the minister, the minister derives his or her powers from the Crown and so, in a real sense, it is the crown whom officials serve and to whom loyalty and duty is owed. (Chapman 1988, 296-7)

This lack of understanding as to whom or what a public servant owes loyalty and duty has produced some difficult situations in recent years. The most instructive case overseas was probably that of Clive Ponting, an Assistant Secretary in the British Ministry of Defence who "leaked" highly classified documents to a member of parliament which he claimed demonstrated that parliament was being deliberately mislead by ministerial statements about the sinking of the Argentinian cruiser

Belgrano during the Falklands conflict. Ponting clearly believed he owed a duty of disclosure to parliament which transcended his duty to his minister or the government. He was tried for treason and acquitted. (Griffith & Ryle 1989, 30-31) The government's response was to issue new guidelines stating the duties and responsibilities of civil servants in relation to ministers which stated in part:

> A civil servant should not decline to take, or abstain from taking, an action because to do so would conflict with his or her personal opinions on matters of political choice or judgement between alternative or competing objectives and benefits; he or she should consider the possibility of declining only if taking or abstaining from the action in question is felt to be directly contrary to deeply held personal conviction on a fundamental issue of conscience.
>
> Griffith & Ryle 1989, 31

The guidelines offer no assistance in situations where an instruction may be improper or illegal, nor does it regard duty and loyalty between minister and official to be in any way reciprocal.

In Western Australia the steady stream of official documents "leaked" to the media has increased in recent years to a flood. The motivation for most of these leaks is almost certainly party political rather than a matter of conscience, duty or the public interest. However, several pertinent issues of a Ponting-like nature, concerning the proper role of public servants have arisen as a result of the Royal Commission's findings.

One of the most interesting concerned John Metaxas, a public servant and former Registrar of Co-operative and Financial Institutions who was found guilty of improper behaviour by the Royal Commission. (RC 12.18.13) Later at a Public Service Commission inquiry Metaxas was found guilty of breaching public service regulations by providing confidential financial information concerning the then President of the Western Australian Liberal Party to both the then Premier and Treasurer, Brian Burke, and another minister, Bob Pearce. Metaxas was suspended by the Commissioner, appealed, and had the finding reversed. There were many mitigating circumstances in this case. One the one hand, the government of the day was under great pressure in parliament as there was a "run" on the funds of a local credit institution, a run alleged to be politically motivated. The information sought for was relevant to this issue. On the other hand, Metaxas, who had been recruited only a short time earlier, had been given no direction, briefings or orientation as to how he should approach his duties as Registrar.

Before passing the information to the Premier, Metaxas noted on the document:

> Much of the information has been passed to me on the understanding that it will not become publicly available. Information provided to the Registry could dry up if it were known that it could at some stage be quoted in Parliament.
>
> (WAIRC 1993, 8)

On appeal, the Public Service Appeal Board decided that: "[T]he Credit Unions Act ... make[s] it quite clear that the Registrar is completely answerable to the Minister in the exercise of '*any* of his *powers*, *authorities*, *duties* and *functions* under this Act'", adding that "In the Boards opinion, Mr Metaxas was doing no more than any public servant at any level would reasonably be expected to do in the circumstances". Finally, the Board added that "Mr Metaxas had little choice other than to comply with the formal request of his minister". (WAIRC 1993, 8,9,10, italics in original)

While this case continues to be in dispute it is clear that, as with the Ponting and other British examples, the problem is more an ethical than a legal one, a situation not helped by the lack of clear guidelines as to how a public servant should interpret his or her duty and loyalty when a ministerial instruction is thought to be improper. That such instructions should be placed in writing if requested would seem to be a minimum requirement if the position of officials is to be safeguarded. Officials for their part should be reminded that in serving their ministers, their zeal should not outrun their discretion.

While the Metaxas case crystalises many of the problems of the relationship between ministers and public servants in the more conventional sense, many of the Burke government appointments were not conventional and are difficult to classify. Many were employed under the *Public Service Act* and were thus officially public servants, but their role and behaviour was quite different. One such instance was Len Brush, accountant, who joined the Policy Secretariat in late 1983 and in mid-1984 was made Chairman of the Superannuation Board, an appointment the Commission asserted, correctly, would "undermine public confidence in appointments to senior Public Service positions".(RC 5.18.9) The Royal Commission found that the Board's "recklessness and dereliction of duty constituted impropriety". (RC 5.17.22) However, the Commission went on to find that:

> primary responsibility for the improper conduct falls upon Mr Brush. He was the Chairman of the Board and, to all intents and purposes, the decision maker in these matters. Mr Brush's approach to the negotiations and sale (of assets) demonstrates gross incompetence and dereliction of duty. His conduct was most definitely improper. (RC 5.17.23)

In relation to the Anchorage Development the Commission found that "Mr Brush should never have been placed in a position of trust". (RC 6.19.5),

Four other senior public servants were charged under the *Public Service Act* when the Commission found they had acted improperly while others were found to have behaved improperly in relation to the collapsed Swan Building Society. In some cases this started a new trend, with those charged appearing before the Public Service Commission inquiry on the arm of a senior lawyer. Neither side found the interpretation of regulations to be unchallengable.

What these instances demonstrated was that above and beyond the obvious need for public servants to serve the minister, theirs is more than a two-person working relationship. Public servants in our system of government are regarded by some authorities as officials in the fourth service of the Crown, that is, comparable to the three armed services. Duty and loyalty to a minister may thus be interpreted as, ultimately, duty and loyalty to the Crown or the Crown's representative. (Chapman, 225, 296) This is to say that in critical matters of public policy, legally and constitutionally public servants are less servants of ministers but, like ministers, more, servants of the Crown. (Griffith & Ryle 1989, 27) This relationship does not appear to have been seriously considered during the Royal Commission's proceedings.

Subsequent to the Metaxas affair a new *Public Sector Management Bill* has been presented to the State parliament. Among other things it seeks to safeguard "the integrity of an apolitical public sector"; have all chief executive officers appointed by the Governor on the recommendation of the minister and "provide for the appointment of all ministerial staff on a separate basis from other public sector appointments". (PSMB(draft) 1993, 4,6,7) In themselves these changes may have made little difference to the Metaxas affair and offer no guidance to public servants who find themselves in similar circumstances. However, they do lead nicely to the remaining section of the discussion.

Ministerial advisers

The final category to be examined on the Fig 4.1 "employee" axis is that which deals with ministerial advisers in both a teleological (situational) and deontological (duty) context. Examples have already been given which illustrate the difficulty of making judgements in this area (pp 82, 89) in relation to the parachuting phenomenon. In Western Australia it is also difficult to establish when a given individual is a public servant or a ministerial adviser as many changed from the former role to the latter. The approach taken here is to deal with them in their more publicly recognisable rather than their official category

In addition, even within the category of adviser there are a number of alternative ways of dealing with this problem of differentiation between senior career public servants, various kinds of ministerial advisers and legislators. Perhaps the most effective way, because of its empirical backing, is that of Aberbach et al (1991, see also Williams 1985) Aberbach's research, began two decades ago and focuses on the background, roles, responsibilities and relationships between high-level bureaucrats and politicians in seven western countries.

The researchers set up four conceptual images of the roles of administrators and legislators and the relationships and division of labour between them. The question the images illuminate is: In what ways are bureaucrats and politicians, as policy makers, similar, and in what ways are they different? (Aberbach et al 1991, 203) The four images assist greatly in analysing the "crime of the employee" question being addressed here.

Image 1 (Policy/Administration) makes the strongest differentiation between senior bureaucrats and politicians in that the latter are seen to set policy and make decisions while the former administer and implement. There is virtually no overlap of function or responsibility between the two, a situation which at senior levels "is unrealistic today, and perhaps always was". (Aberbach et al 1991, 203-04) Nevertheless, in theory it appears closest to what the Western Australian government seems intent on trying to establish.

Image II (Facts/Interests) asserts that bureaucrats and politicians both take part in policy making but whereas bureaucrats focus on facts and the technical aspects of policy, politicians focus on preferences and interests. The policy process here is a shared but highly distinctive responsibility.

Image III (Energy/Equilibrium) portrays both bureaucrats and politicians as engaging in policy making and both are concerned with politics. However, they each serve different constituencies, politicians articulating broad and diffuse interests in society while bureaucrats focus on the narrower interests of organised clienteles. The policy system is energised by *Image III* politicians who seek publicity, raise innovative issues, are more passionate, partisan, idealistic and ideological. *Image III* bureaucrats, on the other hand are prudent, moderate, and risk averse, managing incremental adjustments and providing policy equilibrium. Aberbach's research suggests that *Image III* describes the key differences between bureaucrats and politicians more so than any other although a further image which they develop involves even more overlap.

Image IV (The Pure Hybrid), while being a contradiction in terms, is in some ways a role reversal where bureaucrats would often behave in ways that are characteristic of politicians, while *Image IV* politicians would often behave in ways that overlap with bureaucratic roles. One possible outcome of this image is that central agencies which already enjoy considerable authority have become more important. “Such agencies and their public servants often are at the vortex of the political mediation of policy”. (Aberbach et al 1991, 204-05)

Aberbach et al conclude stating that senior bureaucrats in Australia, as in the United States, are inextricably linked to policy making and political processes – as is the case in nearly all democracies but that they would expect, in cross-national comparisons, civil servants in Australia to look more like the British Civil Servants interviewed for their research. (Aberbach et al 1991, 213)

The Aberbach et al framework for analysis would appear to have great applicability to remarks made above concerning the changing nature of Western Australia's public bureaucracies, including a great increase in the use of ministerial advisers. In Western Australia, as with other systems, the reasons given for these developments are to enhance the political responsiveness of the senior bureaucracy to the executive and also to achieve a higher degree of program efficiency.

While Len Brush's status was a grey area, however, two who were public servants but in reality were “superbureaucrats” were Kevin Edwards and Tony Lloyd. Edwards, a solicitor, was appointed Executive Director (Policy) in the Department of Premier and Cabinet in late 1984 and was later made Deputy Chairman of the SGIC and also a GESB Board member. Edwards was widely known as the de facto Premier and as the Commissioners stated – “We cannot over emphasise the extent of the power and influence wielded by Mr Edwards in discharging his many roles”. (RC 21.1.8) His reputation for toughness spread well beyond the service. Lloyd was a close friend of Premier Burke who had “catapulted” him from local government to be Director of the Policy Secretariat. Lloyd's subsequent appointments were, in the minds of many, excellent examples of why Premier Burke was a poor picker of subordinates. In 1983 Lloyd became Director of the Policy Secretariat and was made Assistant Under-Treasurer from mid-1984 to September 1987, despite opposition from the Under-Treasurer. In March 1987 he was made Chairman of the Government Employees' Superannuation Board, in October he was appointed to Rothwells and later made managing director. He also became a Commissioner of the State Government Insurance Commission, a Director of the WA Development Corporation and a member of the influential Functional Review Committee. Premier Dowding did not disturb the Rothwells-related appointments initially, and went on to strongly infer blame on these two officials for the PICL catastrophe. The unfairness of this judgement merely illustrated how little Dowding understood of the minister-adviser relationship.

Together Edwards and Lloyd were involved at the cutting edge of more deals, negotiations, initiatives and sensitive developments than perhaps even Premiers Burke and Dowding. The two advisers no doubt acted independently on many occasions and they each would seem to fit perfectly Aberbach's *Image IV (The Pure Hybrid)* where senior bureaucrats in this category often are at the vortex of the political mediation of policy. However, this judgement should not be taken to demean the *Image IV* bureaucrat as there is no necessary reason why "Hybrid" behaviour should be in any way unethical. In the case of both Lloyd and Edwards, however, misguided and unethical behaviour did appear to result.

The Commissioners found that Edwards "gave some misleading answers so as to avoid implicating the Government in improper conduct". (RC 21.1.87) He was found to have acted improperly, especially in "translating a general desire by Mr Burke into specific requests of the instrumentalities". (RC 21.1.52), (RC 21.1.29), (RC 21.1.85) Lloyd was found to have "failed to discharge his duties as a managing director" (RC 21.1.49) and to have engaged in "quite extraordinary conduct" for a senior public servant because of the "apparent absence of any relevant notes taken at any time" on a range of matters. (RC 10.26.19)

It is possible to feel some sympathy for these two individuals, more so than with anyone else. Lloyd especially was quite out of his depth by the time of the Rothwells catastrophe. In their favour there was no evidence that any of their actions had been done for personal financial gain – that is, outside of their generous salary packages. The more probable motivation was loyalty to the party, especially Burke, and the exercise of considerable power without significant constraints. While they did not appear to utilise the defence of situational ethics along the lines of Oliver North their actions smacked continually of that kind of reasoning – it worked less and less successfully as the 1980s progressed. In one instance the Commissioners stated that Edwards brought correspondence into existence after the event (an interesting reversal of North's problem); they argued that "This is not conduct to be expected of a senior public servant. Unfortunately, it is conduct which may be induced from a partisan adviser who wrongly considers the end justifies the means". (RC 21.1.39)

Edwards did not recant on any of his past actions saying to the Commission, "A lot of government is really about illusion", and, on a later occasion, that although some decisions by management might be wrong, the people who made them were only trying to do their best, "Their hearts are pure, I'm perfectly satisfied with mine". (*West Australian*, 11 April 1992) He now consults in Hanoi.

Lloyd was later convicted of making improper use of his position as a Director of Western Collieries and was sentenced to two years jail. This was later changed to a $15,000 fine and his conviction was later quashed by the High Court. The Court of Criminal Appeal was to decide if he should be retried. He faces further charges on Rothwells-related matters. (*West Australian*, 21 October 1992) Edwards was fined $10,000 for being knowingly concerned with Lloyd. His conviction was overturned by the High Court.

It is worthy of note at this point that *WA Inc* was just as much a catastrophe for the private sector as it was for the public sector, if not more so. This does not emerge clearly in the Commission's report for obvious reasons. A hint of the wider impact of *WA Inc* is gained from the fact that while the inquiry was concerned with the "commercial activities of government", of the list of 543 witnesses who gave testimony to the Commission 342 or approximately 62% were from the private sector.

Given the lack of any findings of illegal or corrupt behaviour the above discussion, taken together with the evidence from the Royal Commission, makes a strong case for the questionable ethics of some senior employees being a prime cause in bringing about *WA Inc.* But there was a strong situational (teleological) character to the ethics surrounding many of the key actions. While this does not in any way excuse the actions in question, in some cases, had the intended outcome been achieved some of the major players may have been regarded as visionary and feted as heroes. But failure in such situations tends to carry a much heavier penalty than the norm – and rightfully so given the risks taken, in this case, with public assets.

In the next chapter the focus will shift from the judgements made on evidence placed before the Royal Commission to the results of survey research of the senior members of the Western Australia public service. It will be argued that evidence to be presented corroborates the view on the profound impact of unethical behaviour in bringing about *WA Inc*.

References

Aberbach JD, Mexger DB and Rockman BA (1991). Bureaucrats and Politicians: A Report on the Administrative Elites Project. *Aust J Pub Admin*. 50(2) 203-17.

Barker M(1993). The People vs The Executive: The Royal Commission's Recommendations *Brief* March 1993 39-41.

Bogdanor V (ed) (1987). *The Blackwell Encyclopaedia of Political Institutions*, Oxford, Blackwell.

Brazier R (1991). *Constitutional Reform*, Oxford, Clarendon.

Cahill AG (with Overman ES) (1988). Contemporary Perspectives on Ethics and Values in Public Affairs in Bowman JS and Elliston FA (eds) (1988). *Ethics, Government and Public Policy: A Reference Guide*, New York, Greenwood Press, 11-28.

Chapman RA (1988). *Ethics in the British Civil Service*, London, Routledge.

Garrett J (1992). *Westminster: Does Parliament Work?*, London, Gollancz.

Goodin RE (1992). *Motivating Political Morality*, Oxford, Blackwell.

Grabosky PN (1989). *Wayward Governance: Illegality and Its Control in the Public Sector*, Australian Institute of Criminology.

Griffith JAG and Ryle M (1989). *Parliament: Functions, Practice and Procedures*, London, Sweet & Maxwell.

Hailsham Lord (1992). *On The Constitution*, London, Harper Collins.

Harman EJ (1990). WA Inc – Unresolved Issues of Accountability. July, 39pp (Unpublished).

Harman EJ (1992). Public and Corporate Duties: The Lloyd Case in Western Australia *Aust J Pub Admin*. 51(1) March 86-95.

Hayden W (1980). Speech to Institute of Public Administration. *Commonwealth Record*. 24-30 March 425-28.

Haynes A (1992). *Invisible Power: The Elizabethan Secret Services 1570-1603*, Stroud, Alan Sutton.

Kennedy P (1991). Managing the Media in Peachment (ed) op cit, 70-86.

Lawson N (1992). *The View From No 11: Memoirs of a Tory Radical*, London, Bantam.

Lenman BP (1992). *The Eclipse of Parliament: Appearance and Reality in British Politics Since 1914*, London, Edward Arnold.

Mount F (1992): *The British Constitution Now: Recovery or Decline?*, London, Heinemann.

North OL (1991). *Under Fire: An American Story*, London, Fontana.

O'Brien P (ed) (1986). *The Burke Ambush: Corporatism and Society in Western Australia*, Perth, Apollo Press.

O'Brien P and Webb M (eds) (1991). *The Executive State: WA Inc and the Constitution*, Perth, Constitutional Press.

Peachment A (ed) (1991): *The Business of Government: Western Australia 1983-1990*, Sydney, The Federation Press.

Peachment A (1992). Book Review, *AJPA* v 51(1), 137-38.

Ponting C (1985). *The Right to Know: The Inside Story of the Belgrano Affair*, London, Sphere.

Ponting C (1986). *Whitehall: Tragedy & Farce. The Inside Story of How Whitehall Really Works*, Glasgow, Collins.

PSMB (Draft) 1993; Public Sector Management Bill. *Position Paper.* 6pp.

Rees-Mogg W (Lord) and Davidson JD (1991). *The Great Reckoning: How the World Will Change in the Depression of the 1990s*, London, Sidgewick & Jackson.

Richter WL, Burke F and Doig JW (1990). *Combatting Corruption, Encouraging Ethics: A Sourcebook for Public Service Ethics*, Washington, American Society for Public Administration.

Rosen B (1989) *Holding Government Bureaucracies Accountable*, New York, Praeger, 2nd ed.

Schapper P (1993). "Commonwealth State Financial Relations and the Policy Environment" in Peachment A and Williamson J (eds). *Case Studies in Public Policy: A One Semester Work Book*, Perth, Public Sector Research Unit 14-35.

Sinclair I (1975). Speech to Liberal Party Federal Council. Quoted by Ian Marsh: "Policy Making in the Liberal Party: The Opposition Experience" *The Australian Quarterly*, June 1976, 5-17.

Tange Sir A (1982). "The Focus of Reform in Commonwealth Government Administration" *AJPA,* v XLI(1) 1-14.

Taylor R (1993). *Going For Broke: How Banking Mismanagement Lost £Thousands of Billions*, London, Simon & Schuster.

WAIRC (1993). Public Service Appeal Board. *No PSAB 1 of 1993.* 1 April 1993, 10.

Wilenski P (1979) Ministers, Public Servants and Public Policy in *The Australian Qtly.* (June) 31-45.
Williams C (1985). The Concept of Bureaucratic Neutrality. *AJPA* XLIV(1) 46-58.

5

Ethical Behaviour and Senior Public Managers in Western Australia

Allan Peachment

In late 1991 a questionnaire based survey of all 351 members of Western Australia's Senior Executive Service (SES) together with 101 ministerial advisers was undertaken.[1] Composed of 46 questions the survey instrument was divided into six parts: (i) ethical standards within the public sector, (ii) experience of ethical issues, (iii) the *Code of Conduct for Public Servants* (iv) leadership and reform, (v) the role of ministerial advisers and (vi) personal background. A response rate of 45% (158) was obtained from the SES which is acceptable for surveys of this kind. However, only 10 responses were returned from ministerial advisers making that part of the survey statistically irrelevant.

As discussed in earlier chapters, there are a number of individual and situational factors which may influence an individual's decision to behave either ethically or unethically. In this regard all decisions would fall into either a teleological or deontological category.[2] The former category

---

1 My thanks go to the two Public Service Commission consultants who helped devise the questionnaire. Any errors lie with the research team and primarily myself.

2 The term "teleology" comes from the Greek *telos* meaning the end result. Any teleological approach to ethics uses the final result as the standard judgement. On the other hand deontology comes from *deon* for duty. Deontological judgements compare actions to an absolute standard of duty without reference to consequences. These two perspectives may judge the same act differently. For example, if an individual promised not to lie and then did lie, a deontological ethic will almost certainly condemn the action. It violates the duty to keep one's promise. But if the individual lied to bring about a good result, a teleological ethic would not condemn so readily. I am grateful to Roger Wettenhall, Editor of the *Australian Journal of Public Administration* for this clarification.

emphasises outcomes and the latter duty or process. In the field of business ethics one comprehensive study has outlined 254 definitions of ethics expressed in 308 different concepts. These, in turn, have been grouped into 38 categories, the top seven of which are: rules, standards and codes, moral principles, right/wrong in specific situations, belief in social responsibility, what is fair and above board, honesty and telling the truth. (Lewis 1985) This gives some idea of the complexity of the field however, this particular survey dealt with ethical behaviour rather than ethics *per se*.

A technically advanced quantitative and statistical analysis of the survey results, which tested a range of hypotheses, and used descriptive statistics as well as multivariate, factor and discriminant analysis was undertaken by the research team and published separately.(Peachment et al 1994) Brief reference will be made at intervals to this earlier study, however, in this chapter the main focus will be on (i) the analysis of written responses to questions which formed no part of the earlier study and (ii) the presentation of elementary quantitative data from the survey presented in bar-graph form. It must be emphasised that the bar graphs represent only the most simple means of presenting data with no attempt being made to undertake cross-tabulations, for example. Space alone rules out these options.

While descriptive, qualitative analysis of this kind cannot claim statistical validity this need not infer methodological shortcomings. On the contrary, the idea of jointly utilising more than one theory, method or technique in relation to a given research problem has several advantages, including avoiding an over-reliance on single-method measures of concepts. The approach, often referred to as "triangulation", is best expressed in the work of Campbell et al (1959) which suggests that the validity of research findings and the degree of confidence – not only statistical – in them will be enhanced by the deployment of multiple approaches to analysing the problem. (Brannen 1992) The approach recognises that quantitative and qualitative approaches to research have different preoccupations as well as contrasting strengths and weaknesses. For example, the quantitative approach usually emphasises causality, variables, and a heavily pre-structured approach to research, whereas qualitative research is concerned with the elucidation of perspectives, process and contextual detail. (Bryman in Brannen, op cit 64) The idea is to guard against the fact that all forms of measurement are prone to error. (Topping 1955, 1969)

Results

SECTION A: ETHICAL STANDARDS WITHIN THE PUBLIC SECTOR

QUESTION 1: *Explain in your own words the meaning of* "ethical behaviour; within the public sector" *(Please note that we are interested in your perceptions of "ethical behaviour" specifically in the workplace; we are not interested in your broad personal values or moral beliefs (eg, your views on abortion, suicide etc.)*

The result for this question are best interpreted along with the results for question eight – see below. However, it is relevant to note that since this survey was undertaken Denhardt (1991, 274) has made the interesting suggestion of there being three types or levels of ethical responsibility in public administration. First, the democratic foundations of public service ethics where we expect administrators to be responsible, responsive and accountable; second, the managerial foundations where efficiency and effectiveness are emphasised and, finally, the social foundations which includes the principles of justice, fairness, individual rights, equity, respect for human dignity, and pursuit of the common good. The possible application of all three levels concurrently gives an indication of the complexity of the field.

QUESTION 2: *How do you rate the ethical standards of WA public sector employees (in terms of day-to-day operations) in relation to the ethical standards of the private sector? (a) Today, (b) 10 years ago.* The results are shown in Figure 5.1

Figure 5.1: Ethics: Public vs Private

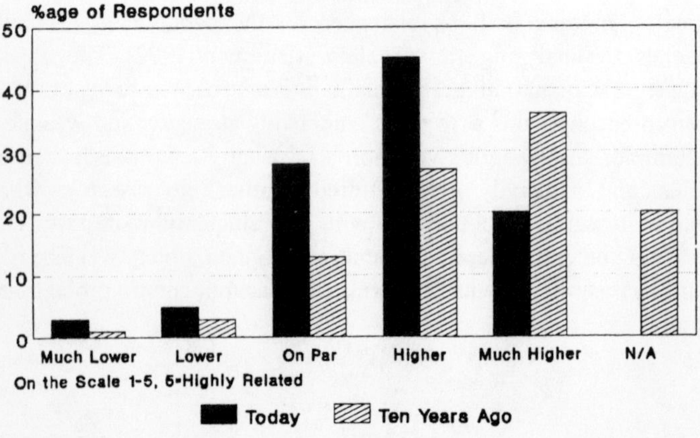

Given the emphasis that the Burke and Dowding governments placed on public sector personnel adopting the values and approaches of business, particularly its more entrepreneurial characteristics, this is obviously a result that raises concerns. It was aspects of this approach, in terms of recruitment from the private sector and training in adopting a private sector managerial outlook, that may need to bear some responsibility for the decline in ethical standards in government. When the two categories of "Much higher" and "Higher" are combined the results depict a lessening of the difference to 14.3% (79.5-65.2) between the two sectors. Given the significant and widely noted decline in private sector ethical standards during the 1980s this may infer a comparatively greater decline for the public sector. While this may be so, there was obviously a strongly held view among respondents that public sector ethical standards were, at the time of the survey, much higher than those in the private sector. This view is not contradicted by the rise of 10% among those who believed that between the two points in time public sector standards had fallen to be "On a par" with the private sector.

QUESTION 3: *How do you rate the ethical standards of WA public sector employees (in terms of day-to-day operations) in relation to the general ethical standards of the wider community? (a) Today (b) 10 years ago.*

Figure 5.2: Ethics: Public Sector vs Wider Community

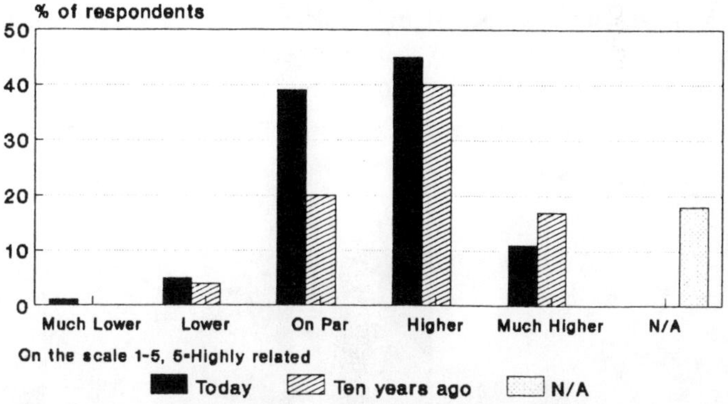

Figure 5.2 suggests that while SES personnel rate the ethical standards of public sector employees higher than those of the wider community, the difference is not as great as that between the public and private sector depicted in the previous question. Nevertheless, a total of 56% (10.7+45.3) indicated that public sector ethical standards were higher or much higher

than the community's standards as against 35% 10 years ago. The "On a par" category had fallen 9.8% (48.8-39) almost identical to the fall in the earlier question. The interesting difference between these two questions is with the category "Lower" which barely registered in the first question but registers 24.4% in the second in terms of the standards of 10 years ago. This dropped to 4.4%, a result which, when interpreted along with the comparable result for question two, suggests that public sector ethical values are seen to be higher today than those of either the wider community or the private sector. While it is understandable for professional groupings to feel ethically superior to some of Perth's entrepreneurial class in the 1980s, it is not so clear why senior public servants should also feel ethically superior to people in the wider community. This elite attitude may be reminiscent of attitudes in the British Civil Service upon which some elements of the public service models itself. (Chapman 1988, Uhr 1991, 288)

QUESTION 4: *Over the period you have worked for the public sector would you say that the ethical awareness and standards within the public sector have: (a) risen considerably, (b) stayed about the same or (c) fallen considerably?*

The mean response to this question was 3.3 – almost mid-scale – which suggests that ethical awareness and standards are believed on average to have "stayed about the same". However, when the full results are revealed (Figure 5.3) the large number of mid-scale responses suggests that the question presented difficulties so that the "decline" category now looks more in line with responses to earlier questions.

Figure 5.3: Variation in Ethical Awareness and Standards During Period of Employment

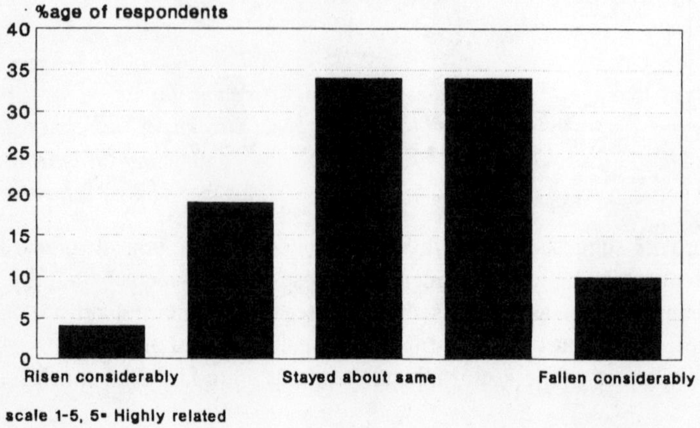

QUESTION 5: *If you believe ethical standards have either risen or fallen could you suggest reasons for this perceived trend? Please limit your reasons to a maximum of three.*

Of respondents who wrote that standards had remained largely the same, one wrote that actual standards on the whole are reasonably good despite some grey areas and that there was a heightened awareness of good standards. Another wrote that most government agencies appear to have made the effort to spell out what is acceptable and that public servants had to evaluate their behaviour. A number thought that while standards were widely perceived to have fallen, this was largely the result of often unfair media publicity. Another believed that public servants were more aware of the need for ethical behaviour in times when it is easy to waver. Finally, one asserted that standards had stayed about the same because of the interplay of demands for higher accountability by the community which pushed ethical standards up, in addition, the ethos of the late 1980s of taking a commercial risk and a preparedness to stretch the law was less acceptable.

Of those who thought that standards had improved the reasons given included – improved accountability measures leading to greater transparency, closer scrutiny, tighter budgets, more formal channels for complaints or grievances, a de-mystification of public sector processes and an increased awareness by the public of public sector costs and outcomes. On this latter point one respondent wrote "Programs and services are developed and delivered with a much clearer outcome orientation. Outcomes are generally articulated within a broad ethical framework". One respondent believed that the reason was the provision of the *Code of Conduct*, another better methods of recruitment and the much greater pressure to perform rather than becoming deadwood; others thought it was due to the increase in media attention, especially investigative journalism and the penetration of television. One gave the reason of "Appalling political behaviour had created the need to set the public service apart from this example", another noted the impact of greater professionalism but added "I discount the few "quasi" public servants temporarily imposed from some areas of the private sector". One noted that standards have risen and continue to rise as the result of deliberate action to heighten ethical awareness and another, better and clearer guidelines from the Public Service Commission, and a third, a higher standard of education and training of public officers.

Finally, on this same question, of the 10 ministerial advisers who responded, six stated that standards had lifted due to the impact of *WA Inc* and Royal Commissions, here and in Queensland, media hype, legislative and work practice improvements, a greater and more positive response to the private sector excesses of the 1980s and a better definition of what is expected and a somewhat better communication of this. Given the low response rate of this part of the sample these particular views cannot be taken as representative.

By far the largest response (48) to this question came from those who believed that standards had declined and that this was linked to ministerial advisers, in one way or the other. The repetitive terms used to express this view included – political jobs for the boys, political appointees, appointment of Labor "friends", politicisation of the public sector (service), parachuting of political appointees, appointment of cowboys and, a government promoted public service culture where looking after your "mates" at public expense became acceptable behaviour. Many of these respondents elaborated their views saying, for example, that *noblesse oblige* was rubbished as old fashioned, that there was a lowered ability to accept the validity of contrary views, and this in an economic and environmental climate which increased the perceived cost of not having one's views prevail; another wrote that one had to be far more devious to achieve anything against the tide of political corruption and interference. A number noted that the ministerial advisers in question did not have the tradition or culture (duties, obligations, loyalties, standards and probity were mentioned by a number of respondents) of public service and had been selectively recruited, poorly inducted and trained. It was said that these people, including some at senior level, had short term agendas and were subservient to ministers' wishes, not the public's well being. This was indicative of a "means over ends" viewpoint. On the same theme another noted that:

> [C]hanges at senior levels have resulted in appointments of people who did not even know how to behave in a legal or moral sense let alone an "ethical" one.

Others pointed to the negative role of outside influences stating that some entrepreneurs and government leaders and politicians were corrupt and that this would flow down the line; another blamed the move away from "Westminster" standards and a poor understanding of public administration.

Others noted the arrogant behaviour and attitude, as well as the lack of leadership from politicians and business leaders. Business people without traditional public sector ethical values, it was said, had taken up senior positions in government and there was an "impression" that promotion was dependent at high levels on not rocking the boat. Associated with this was the apparent belief of some people that they transcended the law and accepted procedures. Selfishness, greed, and bribe takers were terms used by some. One blamed the decline in good ethics on "political interference" and decision making by officers without relevant qualifications and training, of executive decisions made by managers who do not understand technical, scientific or professional problems and issues. In a similar vein another wrote of the rapid expansion of the SES over the past five to seven years and how this produced "younger, politically motivated and less experienced staff". Thus, public servants, s/he wrote, were more often aligned with the ALP than the Liberals and found it more comfortable to support ALP government beyond their usual ethical boundaries. Another wrote that the trend was to provide the advice which senior officers and ministers wanted to hear, whereas previously ministers relied upon departments for advice and the departments were more publicly accountable for advice and records than was the present arrangement with advisers and ministerial staff – it was also alleged that there was an unwillingness on the part of bureaucrats to speak their mind. This attitude led to there being a blurring of the previous distinction between the bureaucracy and the politicians.

This last observation is of course grist to the mill of Aberbach 's remarks on administrative elites mentioned in Chapter 4, but there is more to it than that. The reasons for this vitriolic commentary on ministerial advisers lie not with ministerial advisers alone. Some responsibility must lie with the inadequacy of the executive development programs which have consistently emphasised managerial competencies and omitted any explanation, let alone defence, of the need in modern government for ministerial advisers. It is ironic that a series of Labor governments which saw a need for empathetic and partisan advisers never saw a need to put forward their arguments to those most clearly affected.[3] The relevant academic literature was of course brimming with raw material on the subject of which senior Victorian public servant, Ken Baxter's (1991) article on *Politicisation – Responsiveness* is but the latest excellent example.

QUESTION 6: *How important do you believe the following factors are in influencing public sector employees to behave ethically or unethically? (i) the ethical practices of one's profession (ii) personal financial need (iii)*

3 A former Public Service Commissioner, Frank Campbell, did deliver a brief paper on the topic to a professional meeting in the early 1980s, but there was no follow through.

climate within one's agency (iv) society's moral climate (v) formal government policy and (vi) behaviour of one's peers in the public sector. The results are shown in Figure 5.4

Figure 5.4: Factors Influencing (Un)Ethical Behaviour

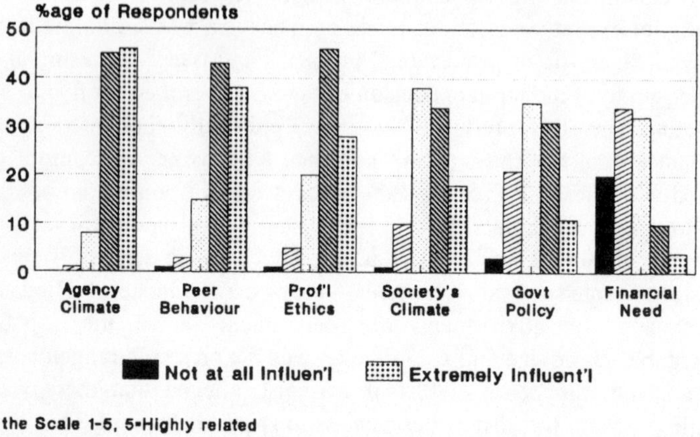

The response to this question, given on a five point scale, made clear that the "climate within ones agency", "behaviour of peers" and "practices of profession" outranked the remaining three factors. This underlines the importance senior managers place on role models such as the behaviour of professional colleagues and civic leaders. This finding relates well to research findings in overseas studies on this question. (See Figure 5.32)

QUESTION 7: *Specify what mechanisms (formal and/or informal) are in place to encourage/promote ethical behaviour in the public sector? (Please list mechanisms and rate each in terms of their effectiveness)*

There was very little focus to responses on this question. The most common response (71) related to peer group influence in all its forms and the importance of professional integrity. The rating for this was in the region of 4-5 where (5) indicated "Highly Effective". By way of contrast the second most common response, the Public Service Commission's *Code of Conduct* (56) rated between 2-3. The *Financial Administration and Audit Act 1985* (FAAA) received 21 mentions and was also rated highly. The remaining responses were a grab-bag of ideas which included the Auditor-General, the Ombudsman, the media, public scrutiny, criminal and other sanctions, training and question time in parliament. There were 12 nil responses.

Much is now written on how to enhance the ethical culture of organisations utilising methods such as a code of conduct, policies, discussion groups, posters, internal publications, training courses and changing external influences. Implemented with care such programs can be very successful (Davidow & Williams 1993) but care should be taken not to be heavy handed:

> By placing all our hopes and attention on developing anti-corruption laws, on developing new and more rigorous accountability and review systems, and on new managerial efficiency techniques, we run the risk of a demoralised and disaffected public service. *Not* because public servants do not want to be accountable and honest. *Not* because public servants do not want to be efficient and provide quality service. Rather it is because most public servants are already honest, responsive and accountable, and these reforms (needed by a few) are viewed as punitive and an insult by the many.
>
> Denhardt 1991, 275

QUESTION 8: *Please indicate to what extent the following are related to your understanding of the term "ethical behaviour"?* Eight factors were presented and the scores they each attained on a five point scale are shown in Figure 5.5.

Figure 5.5: Factors Relating to Ethical Behaviour

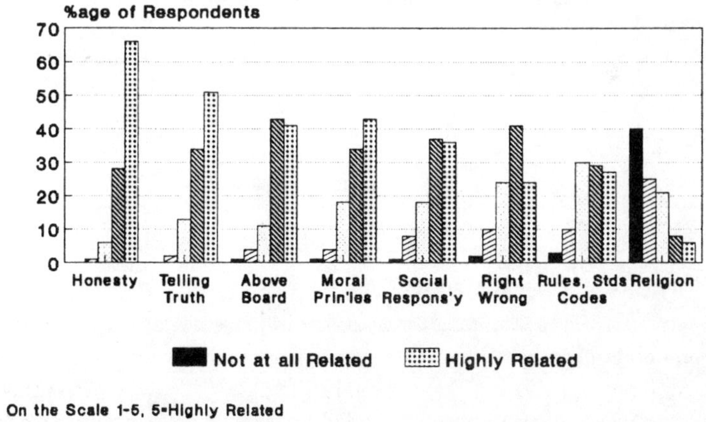

The top two choices are well understood concepts and perhaps such terms should be given more emphasis and usage in case studies. Notably, concepts such as religion come a poor last while formal standards embodied in codes and "situational ethics", as suggested in "right/wrong in specific situations", was not highly regarded. There is not much support here for the Oliver North's of the world.

Section B: Experience of ethical issues

QUESTION 9: *To what extent have you PERSONALLY EXPERIENCED any of the following situations? (1) unfair employment practices (ie jobs for the boys/girls)(2) use of agency facilities for private purposes, (3) concealment of information, (4) leakage of information to outside interests, (5) breach of public sector codes or rules, (6) misuse of government funds, (7) insider information, (8) questionable contracts of government work to outside interests, (9) clandestine relationships between government officials and outside interests, (10) falsification of information, (11) sexual harassment, and (12) gifts/bribes/irregular payments made to or by government agencies.*

The results, depicted in Figures 5.6a and 5.6b, are clearly biased towards the left hand (Never) side of the scale, although several categories; "unfair employment practices", "concealment of information" and "breach of public sector codes" give cause for concern. A more pessimistic view could be taken of these results as, overall, they could be taken to suggest the existence of a small but underlying body of evidence linked to unethical practice observed within the respondents own departments. It should also be noted that as only 10% of respondents were female the responses to the question on sexual harassment are not gender balanced.

Figure 5.6a: Ethical Situations Personally Experienced

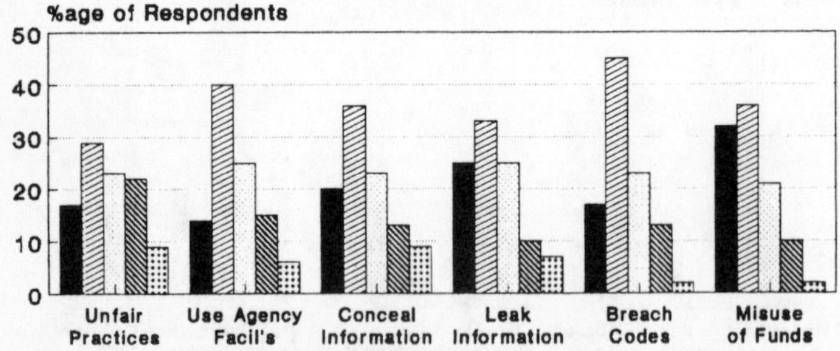

Figure 5.6b: Ethical Situations Personally Experienced

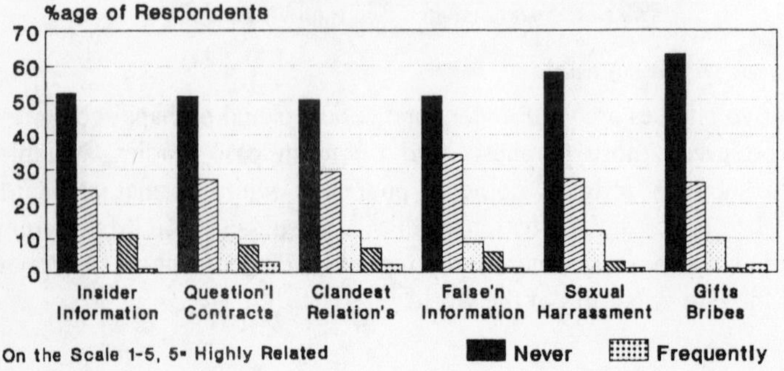

QUESTION 10 poses the same question in general not personal terms. As is usually the case in such circumstances all of the mean values increase and their rank order changes. Figures 5.7a and 5.7b suggest that the underlying body of evidence referred to above increases, together with the resulting concern on unethical practice.

Figures 5.7a: Ethical Situations Generally Experienced

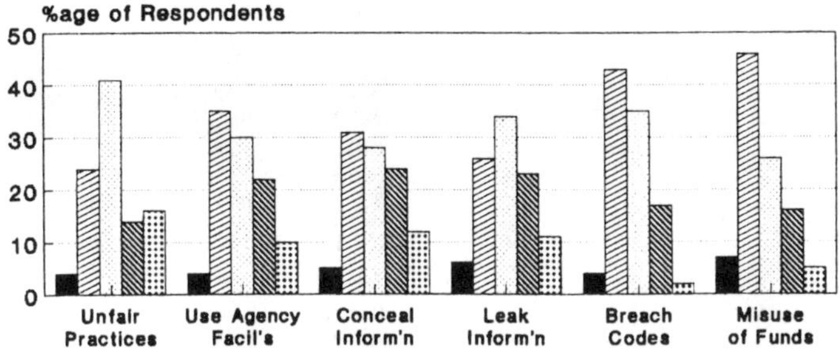

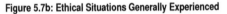

Figure 5.7b: Ethical Situations Generally Experienced

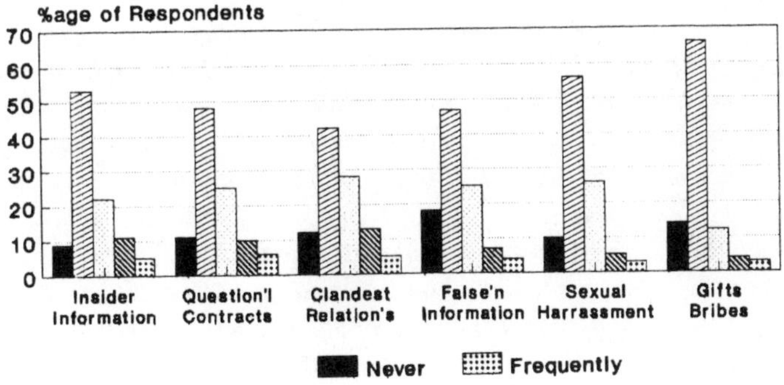

On the scale 1-5, 5=Highly related

QUESTION 11: *How important are the following dimensions to your job?* (1) decision making, (2) leadership, (3) communicating, (4) interpersonal skills, (5) ethics and integrity, (6) delegating, (7) problem solving, (8) organising, (9) training employees.

The results in Figure 5.8 are heavily biased towards the "major part of my job" side of the scale and demonstrate the multi-faceted nature of the public sector manager's role. However, when it is recognised that the list, which is based on surveys in the private sector, deals almost entirely with management related attributes, omitting policy and political skills, the role of the public as opposed to the private manager takes on a deeper complexity.

Figure 5.8: Job Dimensions – Five Most Important

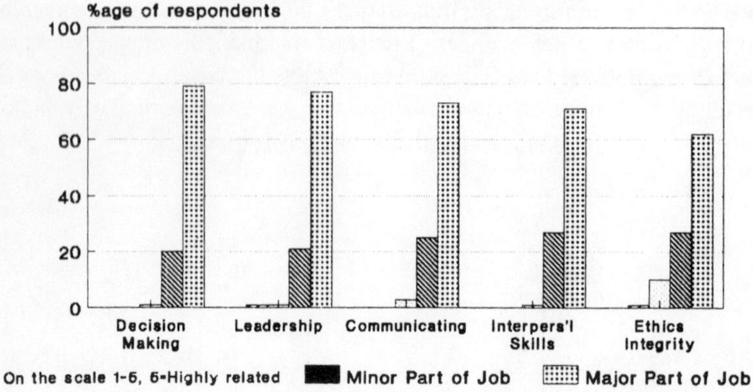

QUESTION 12: *To what extent do you consider the following to be important job requirements? (1) refusal to accept questionable or unethical actions, (2) consideration of the goals, interests and rights of others (eg customers, public employees) when making decisions, (3) not compromising personal standards of behaviour, (4) adherence to laws and regulations when making decisions, (5) making decisions taking account of their long-term effects on society, (6) knowledge of unacceptable and acceptable work practices, (7) provision of accurate and complete information to employees, the public and any concerned others, (8) adherence to established organisational standards of behaviour, (9) willingness to "blow the whistle" on unethical practices, (10) systematic analysis of the ethical or moral ramifications of decisions.* Responses are given in Figure 5.9.

Figure 5.9: Important Job Requirements

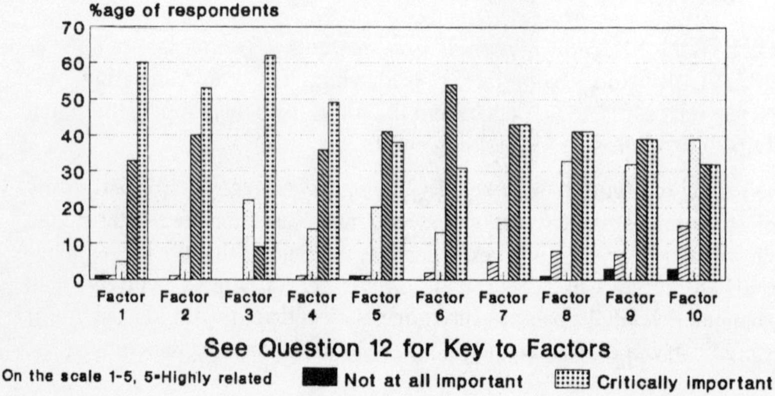

Again, the responses are strongly biased towards the "critically important" side of the five point scale thus making the senior managers role more complex when earlier questions are taken into consideration. Factors one and three: "refusal to accept questionable or unethical actions" and "not compromising personal standards of behaviour" rate particularly highly. However, factor nine, "willingness to 'blow the whistle' on unethical practices" rates a total of only 10% on the two left hand points of the scale and, as the factors listed are shown according to their mean value, this suggests that whistle blowing is not well received or is looked on as a risky activity, which it is. There is obviously room for some formal career safeguards in this area.

QUESTION 13: *Indicate which of the following statements best describes the situation within your Agency. (circle* one *number only)*

The pressure to compromise my personal ethics and conform to Agency expectations is:

There is no pressure to conform	33%
Relatively weak and becoming weaker	5%
Relatively weak and staying the same	33%
Relatively weak but becoming stronger	13%
Relatively strong but becoming weaker	1%
Relatively strong and staying the same	12%
Relatively strong and becoming stronger	3%

The results are given in Figure 5.10.

Figure 5.10: Pressure to Compromise Personal Ethics

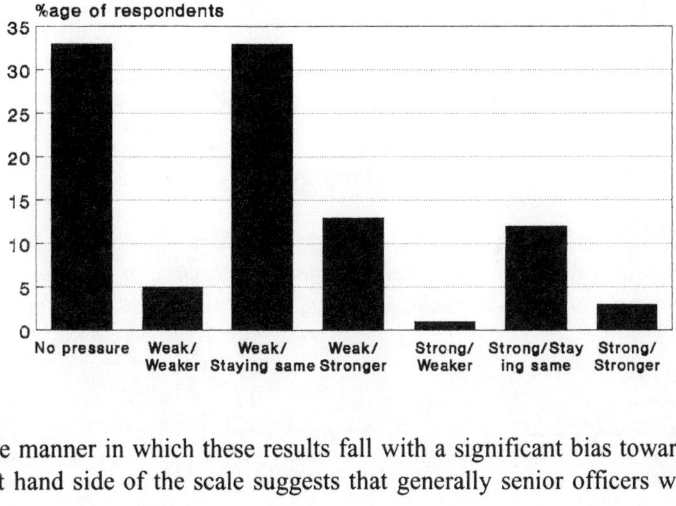

The manner in which these results fall with a significant bias towards the left hand side of the scale suggests that generally senior officers work in situations where their own ethical values prevail with little pressure to compromise. The three responses on the right hand side of the scale, however, totalling approximately 16%, give cause for concern depending in which departments or agencies respondents are located. If a significant proportion of them work in central agencies or more policy sensitive departments then the overall ethical impact may be more serious than the figures suggest.

QUESTION 14: *Looking back no more than five (5) years, how often have you faced a conflict between what you believe was right according to your personal ethics and what was expected of you by your agency?*

If the results of this question (Figure 5.11) are interpreted alongside those of the previous one then there is rather more cause for concern. For, in more general terms, the frequency of conflict between personal and agency ethics suggests that either the conscience of senior officers is not sufficiently robust or that questionable actions are being demanded of them by ministers and others.

Figure 5.11: Frequency of Conflict Between Personal and Agency Ethics

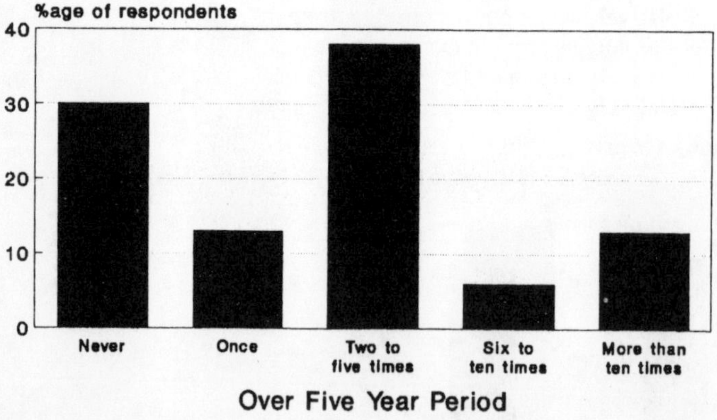

QUESTION 15: *If a minister, ministerial adviser, or a more senior officer, instructs you to take an action which you believe to be contrary to the* Code of Conduct for Public Servants, *would you point out to him/her that it is so?*[4]

---

4 *The Code of Conduct for Public Servants* (Perth, Government Printer) was first issued in 1988 (Its official title is: *Rights, Responsibilities and Obligations: A Code of Conduct for Public Servants).*

Figure 5.12: Would Point Out that Action is Contrary to Code of Conduct for Public Servants

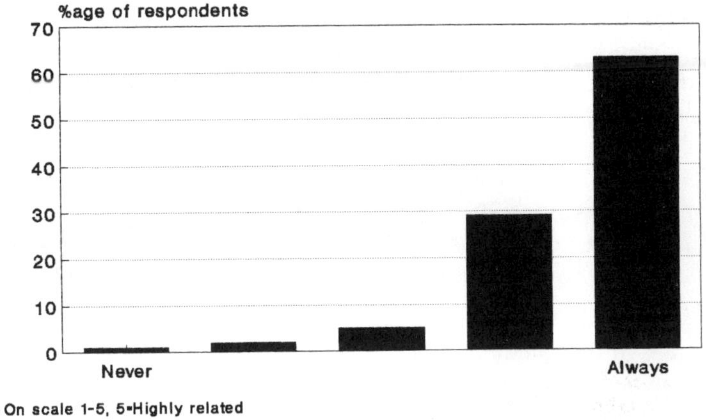

Figure 5.13: Would Again Refuse Instruction to Carry out Action

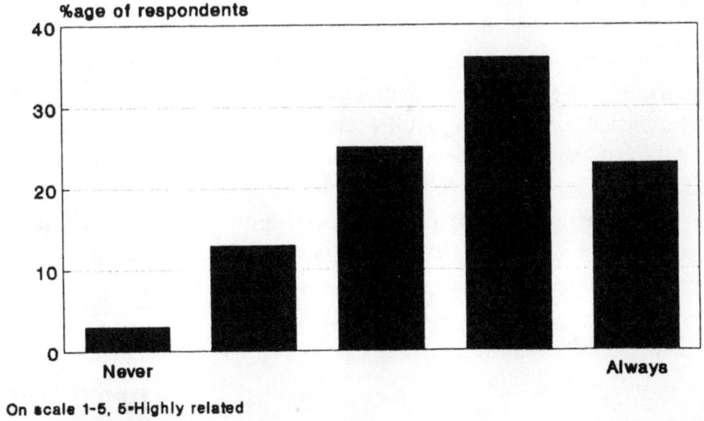

Figures 5.12 and 5.13 profile a senior officer who, when instructed to undertake action which in her view might breach official guidelines, believes she would give frank, fearless advice in relation to the instruction as demanded by the traditions of the service. While the advice in question would not necessarily be repeated if the instruction was again given, the situation portrayed intimates that there is potential for a clash of wills when there is conflict between personal-official and ministerial ethics. However, when QUESTION 16 is posed: *If you were still instructed to*

carry out this action, would you refuse? understandably many senior officers would bend to the will of the minister. Of course, much may depend on the calibre of the minister giving the instruction, a junior minister may be contested for a second time, but if the minister is the Premier, as in the Metaxas case (Chapter 3), the shift to the left of the scale would probably increase considerably.

QUESTION 17: *In your daily work situation whom or what do you regard yourself as serving? (Please rank the following list, with 1 representing the most important and N/A representing not applicable: The Minister, The Government, The Crown, The Parliament, The Public and, Other (explain).*)

The results of this question (Figure 5.14) further muddy the waters in the sense that the first four options – Minister, Other, Public and Government – received similar scores. It is surprising that so many respondents selected "other" from the list of options, falling as it does almost equal with "Minister" and ranking higher than "public", to say nothing of parliament. This reflects harshly on the government's much vaunted "whole of government" policy which sought to break down this kind of departmentalism. "Other" in this instance included "Board of management", "Health Department employees", "Staff", "Department", "Government Agencies", "Chief Executive Officer" and "Sector of the public". Given the earlier discussion, the low choice of the Crown bears out the obscure meaning attached to that concept, indeed one respondent wrote "The question is academic nonsense, grow up". However, replies from the Auditor-General's Department, among others, made a clear link between that office and service to the Crown, as they should.

Figure 5.14: Whom/What Do You Serve?

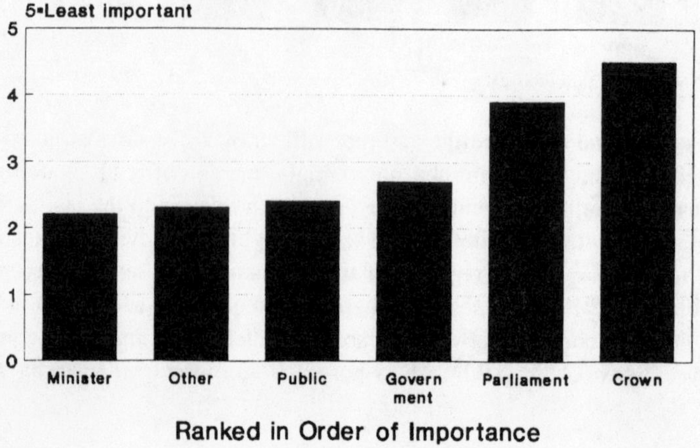

QUESTION 18: *If you face an ethical dilemma in your work situation is there somewhere or someone to whom you can go, in the public sector for advice? (Please specify position/title, and limit your examples to a maximum of two.)*

Responses to this question revealed the existence of a most unsatisfactory state of affairs. For example, 38 replies gave a straight "no" which says little for the quality of established support systems. This was balanced by the 25 who nominated the Public Service Commissioner, Dr Michael Wood, as their choice of adviser. This suggested a relationship in which a measure of trust and integrity prevailed. However, this was undermined by those few who nominated the Public Service Commission or its officers, but specifically rejected the Commissioner. One wrote that s/he would not go to either the Public Service Commissioner or the director of his office of Merit Protection "because of the lack of trust and ethics due to the politicisation of the public service". Another respondent endorsed this saying, "The office of Public Service Commissioner is too embroiled in the politics of the system". A third wrote of having "little trust in the 'top brass'." The negative tone was unexpected; such views were believed to exist among senior managers but the question did not request reasons.

Among the remainder of the responses a number nominated their own Commissioner, several mentioned senior members of Crown Law, in one case the Chief Justice. Others mentioned the Auditor-General, the Ombudsman, the Official Corruption Commissioner and professional peers. There were 11 "Nil" responses.

QUESTION 19: *How would you regard the behaviour of a public service employee, who, in encountering an ethical crisis in his/her public sector duties, makes that crisis public knowledge?*

There was very little response to the extremes of this scale, the bulk of the response being evenly divided about the mean (2.9). (Figure 5.15) This result suggests that executives are divided in their view on how to react in these circumstances and it follows from this that "whistle blowers" should not expect automatic approval from colleagues and peers for what they may regard as high minded actions. If whistle blowing is to be encouraged, or at least safeguarded for purposes of ensuring good ethical practice then guidelines need to be clearer for those considering the action.

One interesting response to this question stated: "The question is deceiving! First the crisis should be dealt with internally and by reference to power figures in the public service or ministry. Failing these and given the issue is not petty I would suggest that the employee has a greater accountability". The respondent, who appeared to have well developed political and constitutional antennae, did not say whether that "greater accountability" was to the public interest or even the Crown.

Figure 5.15: Making Ethical Crisis Public Knowledge

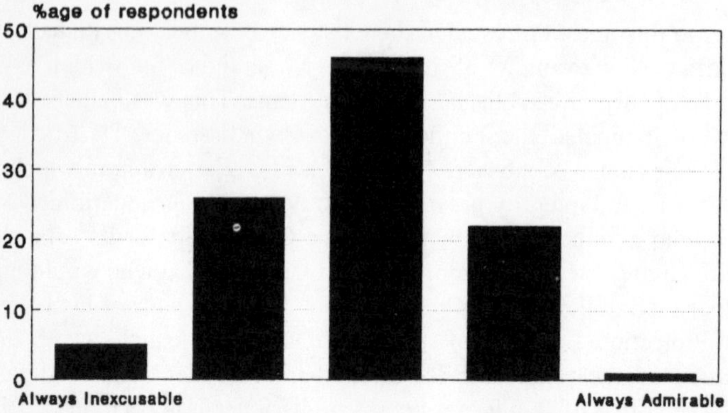

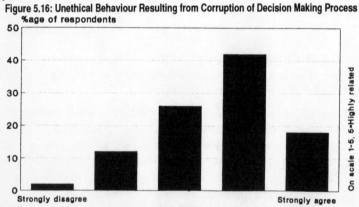

QUESTION 20: *Unethical behaviour would be assumed to originate from individuals whose ethics have been corrupted in some way. However, such behaviour may also originate from the corruption of a rigorous decision-making process. For example, some-one may deliberately by-pass formal mechanisms in order to achieve set objectives. Would you agree that this may sometimes be the case?*

Figure 5.16: Unethical Behaviour Resulting from Corruption of Decision Making Process

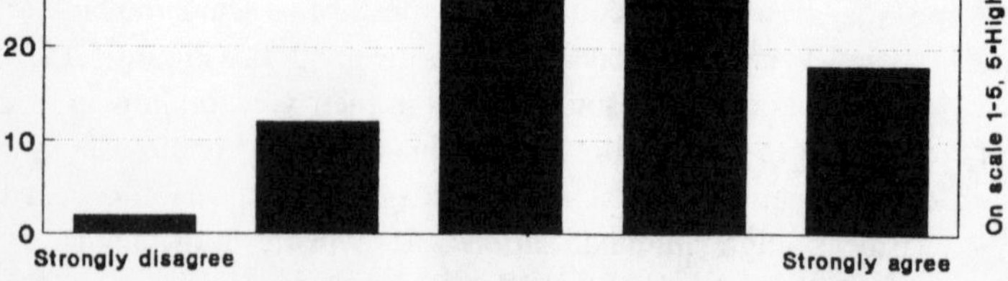

Figure 5.16 portrays considerable support for this suggestion and the notion that ends over means does prevail in some instances. It was the apparent search for a means to by-pass formal mechanisms, even the parliament in some instances, that became the *bête noire* of Labor's decision-making processes in the 1980s.

Part C: The code of conduct for public servants

QUESTION 21: *Are people in the public sector generally aware of the Code of Conduct for Public Servants? (ie is the Code discussed amongst public sector staff?*

QUESTION 22: Have you personally read the *Code of Conduct for Public Servants?*

The response to these questions does not reflect well on the relevance, availability (it was not a readily available document) or the "marketing" of this code. Its overall lack of impact at senior levels indicates low effectiveness. (Figure 5.17) An unimpressive 77% of respondents claimed they had read the code and, when asked in QUESTION 24 if the *Code* assisted in influencing ethical behaviour in the public sector, the result (Figure 5.18) endorsed the view given in the ethics literature, that *Codes of Conduct,* whether in the private or the public sector, are relatively ineffective. (Smith & Carrol 1984; see also Peachment et al 1993)

Figure 5.17: Awareness of Code of Conduct for Public Servants

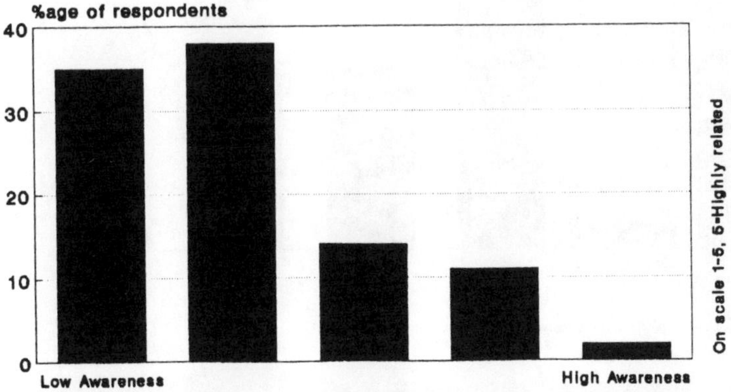

Figure 5.18: Influence of Code of Conduct for Public Servants on Ethical Behaviour

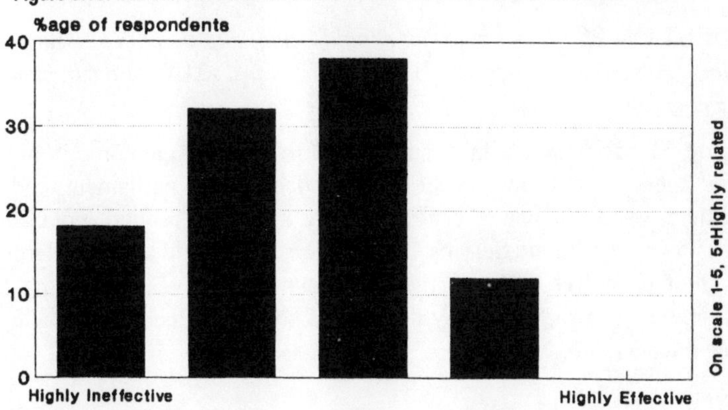

Part D: Leadership and reform

QUESTION 25: *Is unethical behaviour a problem in the public sector?*

While opinion was again divided on this question (Figure 5.19) the majority did not see such behaviour as a serious problem. This result may appear to clash with some of the responses given so far (and some to come) and this points to the difficulty of relating the various responses one to the other and the need to engage in rather more sophisticated cross-tabulations and other forms of analysis. In a qualitative sense the question of context and levels of analysis would also assist in acquiring a wider understanding.

Figure 5.19: Unethical Behaviour as Public Sector Problem

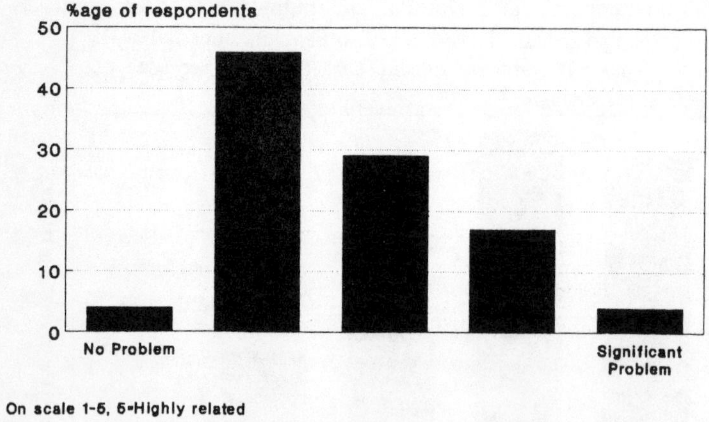

QUESTION 26: *To what extent should leadership on ethical issues come from: (1) Your line agency, (2) State politicians, (3) State parliament, (4) a central agency?*

Figure 5.20 reveals that most support is for leadership to come from one's own agency or from outside the service – the parliament and, or, politicians, rather than a central agency such as Premier and Cabinet, Treasury or the Public Service Commission. This could also be interpreted as chief executive officers, the respondents, merely safeguarding their empires by ensuring that they themselves remain influential in matters of ethical leadership.

Figure 5.20: Desired Source of Leadership on Ethical Issues

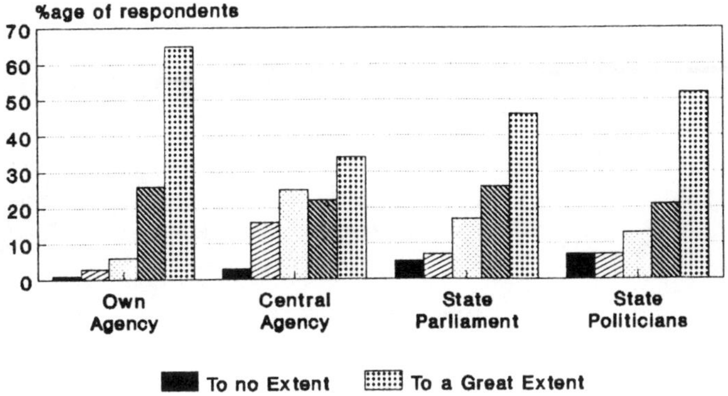

While the parliament did not figure prominently in the previous question, when asked in QUESTION 27 *By what means do you think* State parliament *could take a more prominent role in helping resolve or investigate ethical matters? (1) Joint House committee, (2) House committee, (3) Allotting time for discussion, and (4) Council committee.* the response became more focused. (Figure 5.21) Respondents preferred any significant role to be taken by a joint committee of the parliament, showing scant regard for either of the individual houses or in allotting more time for debate on ethical matters. The response is hardly surprisingly given the circumstances of recent years.

Figure 5.21: State Parliament's Role in Resolving Ethical Matters

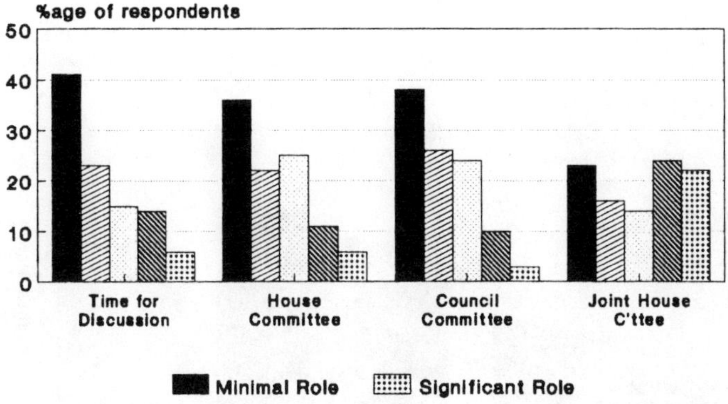

QUESTION 28: *Would you regard private enterprise in WA as setting an ethical standard or role model for the public sector* 6% of respondents replied yes, 86% no, and 8% do not know. The results are depicted in Figure 5.22 which, apart from clearly displaying the derisiveness with which the suggestion was greeted, clearly demonstrates the disfavour with which private sector ethics are regarded in the public sector. The government's intention to introduce private sector style managerialism into public sector management would not fare well against such entrenched antagonism.

Figure 5.22: Private Enterprise as Ethical Role Model

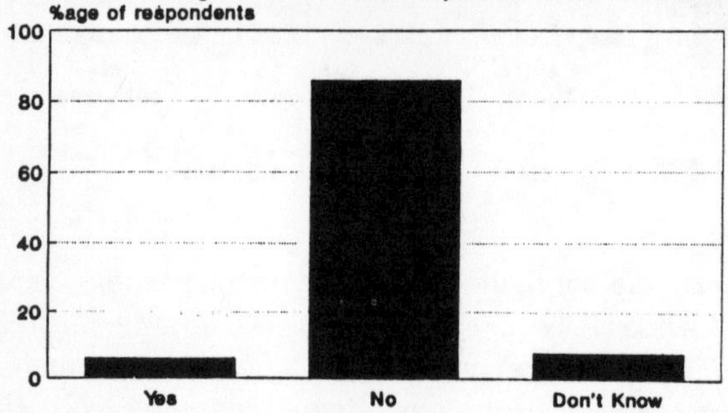

A more equivocal response was given to QUESTION 29: *An ethics audit examines the ethical practices of departments in a manner comparable with the auditing of financial practice. How important do you consider the use of ethics audits as a means of monitoring ethical standards?* This result (Figure 5.23), when linked with others, such as the response given to QUESTION 27, may suggest that neither political institutions such as parliament, nor techniques such as ethics audits are seen as a key to good ethical practice. The emphasis favoured by respondents appears to fall more frequently on intangibles such as the inculcation of greater honesty, integrity and the trust attached to close relationships with professional colleagues in the service.

5.23: Monitoring Ethical Standards via Ethics Audits

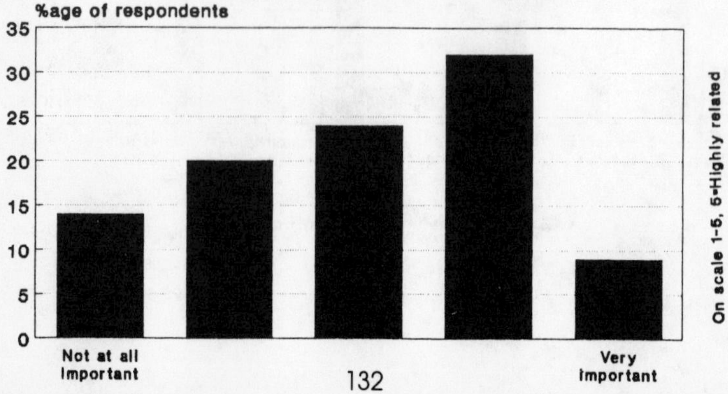

QUESTION 30: *In the widest context, what steps, if any, do you believe need to be taken to reduce problems of an ethical nature in the public sector? Please limit your examples to a maximum of four.*

This was a very open ended question and was anticipated to draw a very wide range of options and suggestions. However, a preliminary examination showed that the role of ministerial advisers had, once again, figured more prominently than any other single factor. Thus, it was felt that these particular responses should be given special attention. In order to establish some mode of categorisation it was decided to cross tabulate all 158 responses from the entire survey according to how each respondent had answered QUESTION 32. This question was selected because it had specifically addressed the question of ministerial advisers, asking:

In terms of influence over the minister do ministerial advisers have far too little or far too much influence?

Responses to QUESTION 32 were to be given on a five point scale with (1) indicating "Far too little influence". The 158 responses were divided according to where on the five point scale the respondent had answered. It was felt that this approach effectively categorised the intensity of feeling of each response thus allowing a more perceptive analysis.

Proceeding along these lines, the 60 responses to QUESTION 30 which fell on point (4) together with the 60 (making a total of 120) on point (5) ("Too Much", or "Far Too Much Influence Over the Minister") of QUESTION 32 were grouped together. It is the responses which these 120 make in relation to reducing problems of an ethical nature concerning ministerial advisers upon which this analysis initially concentrates.

There were several calls for a return to the allegedly pre-1983 career based non-politicised public sector and the need for ethical leadership at both a political and senior officer level. Others wanted to see better examples of ethical behaviour set by State parliament and parliamentarians, by politicians and ministers and by CEOs and central agencies. As one respondent wrote – "Start with the CEOs and SES, if it is not there you have lost". There was one suggestion for the creation of a public service ethics ombudsman who would report to the Governor, another suggesting that "ethics panels" be established while a third respondent advocated the setting up of an independent body, perhaps quasi-judicial or headed by the Chamber of Commerce and Industry, to which people could respond with major ethical issues. There was an interesting call for the institution of programs through which public servants could "talk" out ethical problems. Some suggested that politicians, ministerial staff and public servants should sign an "ethics commitment" and that better ethics could be achieved by building quality into corporate cultures. A number wanted either the Auditor-General's independence from Treasury enhanced or the agency's staff numbers and mandate increased. Others wanted protection for whistle blowers – dobbers as one wrote – for officers refusing to obey improper or unethical instructions, as well as for the immediate passage of freedom of information legislation, more open than that proposed at the time. One unusual suggestion was to provide public recognition and, or, reward officers who made exemplary contributions towards the good standing of the public service; a view shared by another who sought public recognition for the high principles of the public service. On the other hand one suggested penalising public servants who have second jobs outside the public sector or who may partake in business interests. Several wanted CEOs to be able to hire and fire and a reduction in security of employment, but another, more interestingly, sought to ensure that all high level entrants both understood and embraced public service ethics.

As foreshadowed, this larger group of respondents was more outspoken about the widely regarded negative role of ministerial advisers, seeing them generally as a "grey area" and a serious threat to good government. Commonly expressed views on advisers included the following: reduce political influence/ interference/ parachutists, cease/ eliminate political or favoured appointments, depoliticise senior appointments, remove all political intermediaries and ensure that jobs for the boys and girls and the use of high cost consultants by ministers are eliminated. There was a widefelt need for the roles of ministerial advisers and the relationship between them and CEOs to be clearly spelled out. Another wanted the role of both ministers and ministerial advisers to be better defined and limited to policy. Presumably, they were not to involve themselves in management issues. Elaborating on this, one respondent wrote "Ministers need to trust advice from departments instead of setting up their own bureaucrats in the minister's office who attempt to give orders to public servants when they have only a superficial understanding of the issues". This was obviously a sore point as another wrote, "Bar ministerial advisers from giving direct instructions to departments and agencies". One slightly obscure response advocated breaking up the service.

Still on the question of ministerial advisers it was suggested that they either (i) be appointed from within ranks of permanent public servants or

(ii) if appointed from outside on a term with the minister – make sure that term finishes when the minister's does. Some urged a reduction in the influence of political expediency on decision making, a view that might align with the call for there to be an ethics "phase" inserted in all policy development and projects. Revealing a little more drama some called for less political control of the bureaucracy, the elimination of censorship from annual reports and a cleansing and stabilising of the service.

Others blamed poor ethical practice on central agencies for their lack of leadership and wanted the role and influence of the Ministry of Premier and Cabinet on the public sector and its operations reduced. In terms of agency action one wanted frank discussion both encouraged and convened by the Public Service Commission (PSC) and for the Commission to lead by example and make hard-nosed decisions about unethical behaviour within its own portfolio. Another wanted a strong and determined push by an apolitical PSC to market the needs for higher ethical standards to be adopted. Finally there was the interesting suggestion calling for the registration of all senior officers with financial interests and political affiliations and for the disclosure of donations and appointment to positions. The most appealing response was from the officer who wrote that the step to be taken in order to reduce problems of an ethical nature in the public sector was the publication of findings of surveys such as this.

Of the 38 remaining replies, 37 were located on the mid-point (3) of the five point scale of question 32 and one on point two. None was located on point one. Seven of these replies gave no written response to question 30 and a collage of the remainder is as follows.

One respondent believed that there were no significant ethical problems in the public sector while another believed that such a problem was easily exaggerated and that to begin an accurate assessment the problem is best addressed at agency level. A third believed that ethical problems could be reduced by starting with "small things", not using employers' time and resources for private purposes thus setting examples at all levels.

Many respondents in this group stated that ethics should be given a higher profile by being written into the job description, by setting an example, by undertaking awareness programs and through the *Code of Conduct.* One noted that the PSCs guidelines should contain examples of (in)appropriate behaviour and that there should be documented rules of behaviour for politicians. Another urged that public servants should be cautioned against getting into situations in which conflicts of interest or temptation may arise. This might require putting into suitable legislation the instruction that ministerial directions to both authorities and executive officers should be in writing, consistent with enabling legislation and recorded in the annual report. One individual made the novel suggestion for the staging of hypothetical examples of potential conflict within particular agencies and within particular sectors, a kind of action case study. There were calls for institutional ethics committees or a small advisory group to senior executives, in teaching hospitals for example, dealing with patient care. Many emphasised the importance of both training and education as well as leadership and communication. Some others stated a preference for more open decision making and the use of ethics audits and greater accountability – there is almost none now, noted one.

More specific measures recommended included, the reintroduction of loyalty to the service, the retention of all documentation for a reasonable period of time, for the PSC to deal severely with instances of serious unethical behaviour and to punish breaches. Another urged the facilitation of procedures for the removal of unethical or non-performers from the public service. Others demanded higher standards of behaviour from political masters, business leaders and professional groups, the jailing or sacking of offenders, the return of funds and heavy fines. Further, the highest possible number of convictions from the then current royal commission and the further investigation of the State's parliamentarians and senior public servants who have been mentioned on the fringes of *WA Inc*. A number urged the elimination of party hacks, political appointees and failed advisers perhaps perceiving that the problem stemmed from the inability of advisers to separate political from other functions. It was suggested that ministerial advisers should be made responsible and accountable for their decisions and that they make their decisions identifiable.

The final piece of advice from this group was that the post of Public Service Commissioner should be a non-political appointment and be responsible to parliament, this, it was argued, would limit political appointments and patronage which were seen to have been rife in the service in recent years reflecting the *WA Inc* foul-ups.

E. The role of ministerial advisers

This section of the survey proved to be controversial in a number of ways. QUESTION 31 asked: *How well do you consider the minister, within your agency, is served by his/her ministerial adviser(s)?* Figure 5.24 gives a mixed but somewhat negative signal in response to this question and there is obviously much room for greater uniformity in perceptions as well as, perhaps, reality.

Figure 5.24: Service Given to Ministers by Ministerial Advisers

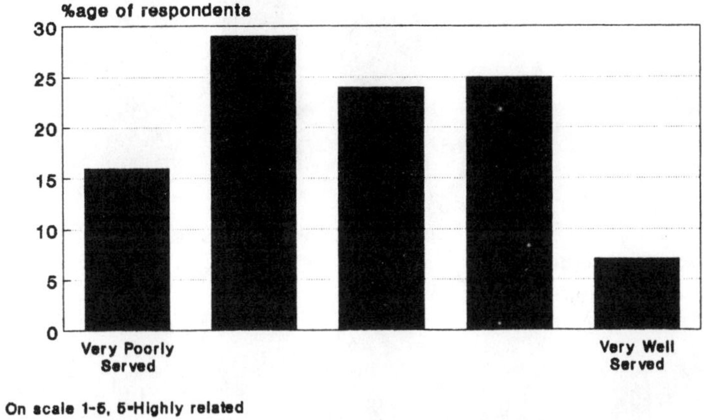

This is especially so when the response to QUESTION 32 is considered. This question was aimed more generally and asked: *In terms of influence over the minister do ministerial advisers have: far too little influence* or *Far too much influence.* Ministerial advisers were seen as having far too much influence over ministers and, as with so many responses in this section, was a severe rebuff to the Labor government, particularly those ministers and advisers who first set these reforms in motion. (Figure 5.25) As will be seen, the apparent lack of regard in which advisers were held suggests that it was they (with some significant exceptions) who, in addition to select senior ministers, were held responsible for the apparent catastrophic collapse of ethical values in the public sector during the Burke-Dowding years. Responses to some of the following questions offer support to this view.

QUESTION 33: *To what extent would you regard the following as being the proper role(s) of ministerial advisers? (1) ensuring the consideration of all policy options, (2) ensuring the minister receives all necessary information, (3) preventing the concealment of alternative policy options, (4) looking after the minister's party political interests, (5) ensuring the full implementation of ministerial directives, and (6) overcoming resistance within the bureaucracy.*

Figure 5.25: Influence of Ministerial Advisers Over Ministers

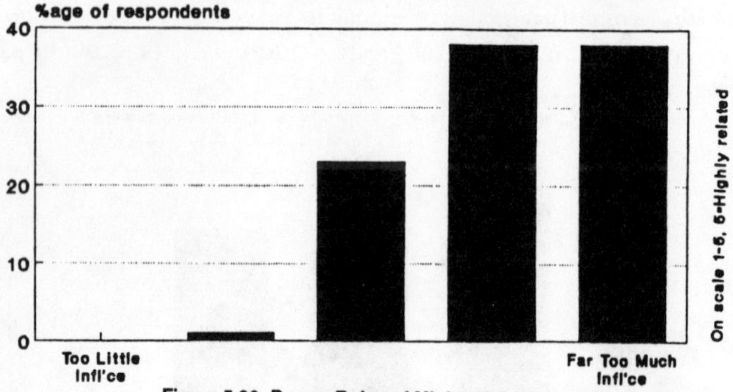

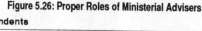

Figure 5.26: Proper Roles of Ministerial Advisers

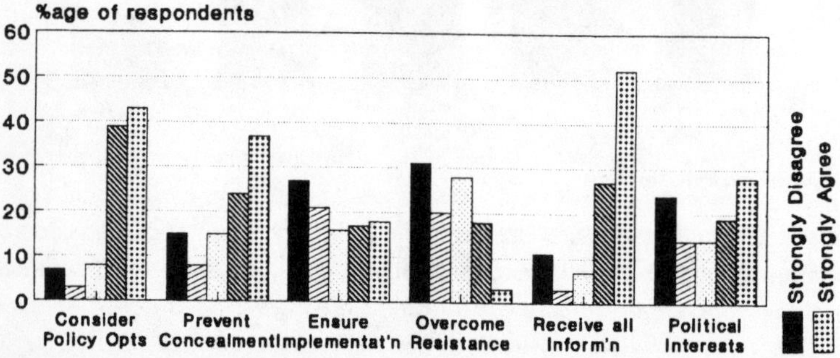

While not exhaustive the above options are well known in the literature as reasons for employing ministerial advisers in modern government. (Chapter 4) The results (Figure 5.26) suggest that senior officers are both aware of and comfortable with most of these reasons and regarded some as constituting a "proper role". They showed most opposition to the view that such advisers were intended to help "overcome resistance within the bureaucracy"; most probably this did not reflect well on their own professionalism despite such resistance being well documented. (Chapter 4) However, their relatively wide acceptance of the adviser role did not prevent extensive and intense criticism of the outcomes in practice.

QUESTION 34: *What is your opinion regarding the number of ministerial advisers in (a) your agency and (b) the minister's office?* While many respondents sat on the fence in this instance, there was clearly disquiet concerning the numbers of advisers, more so in the minister's office than in the agency itself. (Figure 5.27) In each case the numbers were seen as excessive providing a basis for both the souring of relations and for making allegations of waste.

Figure 5.27: Number of Ministerial Advisers in Office/Agency

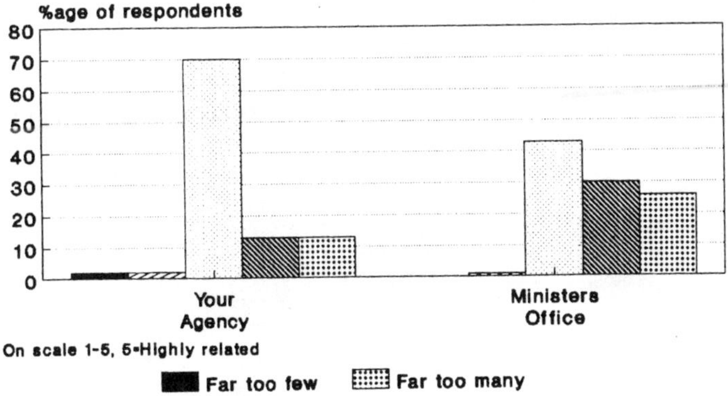

QUESTION 35: *What impact does the presence of ministerial advisers have on the ethical standards of public servants?* Figure 5.28 endorses this view, making a very strong statement against the impact advisers are alleged to have on the ethical standards of public servants. This response, when linked to others, points to a huge communication-educational chasm between the government's intentions in introducing the adviser system in the first place, and how it was perceived by those who saw it in operation at first hand.

5.28: Impact of Ministerial Advisers on Ethical Standards

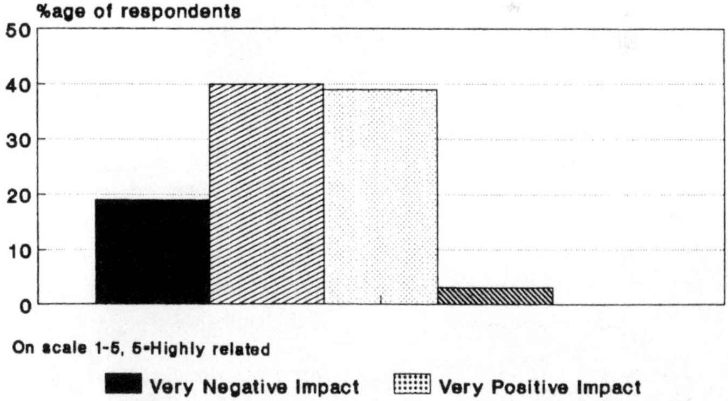

In Section E two questions were intended to be answered by ministerial advisers only however, as already mentioned, only 10 advisers responded to the survey. The two questions were: QUESTION 36: *Do senior officials help you serve the minister?* and QUESTION 37: *In terms of influence over the minister, do senior officials have minimal influence or too much*

influence? Unfortunately, such a low response rate must be disregarded. It could be that in deciding (or more likely being instructed) not to answer the questionnaire, advisers have been prevented from defending their position.

Finally, the demographic data of respondents revealed that, on average, they had worked in the public sector for 21 years (Figure 5.29) and in that period had worked for 3.5 agencies. In addition 61% had worked in the private sector for an average of 8 years. Only 10% of respondents were female. For the overall age and qualifications profiles see Figures 5.30 and 5.31.

Figure 5.29: Time Period Worked in Public Sector

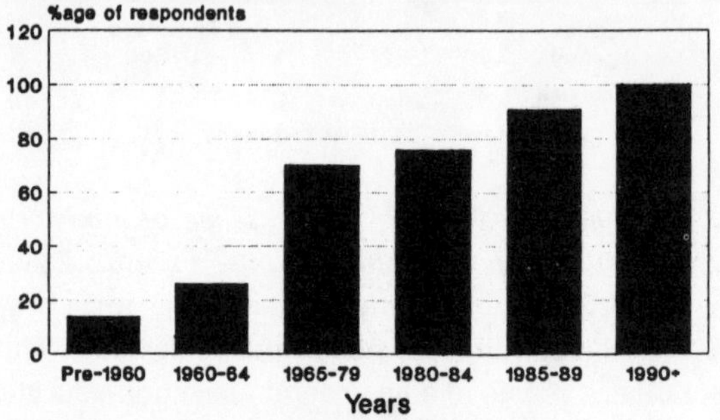

Figure 5.30: Age Profile

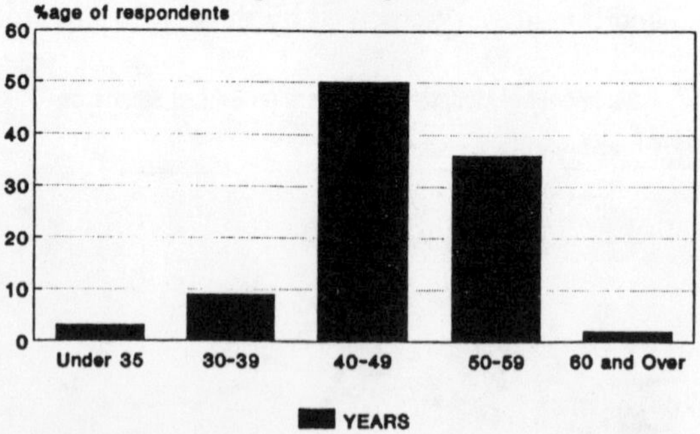

Figure 5.31: Highest Educational Qualification Attained

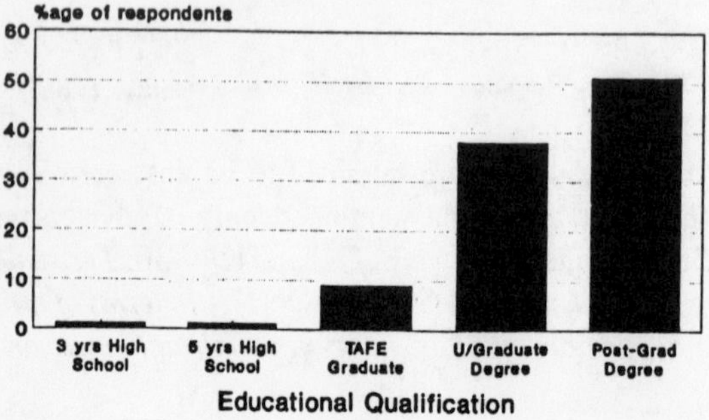

Some international comparisons

It will be recalled that QUESTION 6 of the survey asked how important respondents believed six listed factors were in influencing public sector employees to behave ethically or unethically. Most of the listed factors were extracted from similar surveys of ethical behaviour in the United States taken as far back as 1961, while one was a survey of the private sector in Western Australia which was undertaken in 1991. (Soutar et al 1991) The close identity of most of the listed factors allowed comparisons to be made both over time and between Australia and the United States and the public and private sectors in Western Australia. Comparisons between the five separate studies are set out in Figure 5.32 where it can be seen that the rankings bear a strong similarity. When these results are placed on a bar graph which shows the means values for each study and for each factor it can be seen that on all factors where comparisons can be made, the Western Australian results, both public and private sector, have the highest mean value.

Figure 5.32: International Comparisons 1961-1992

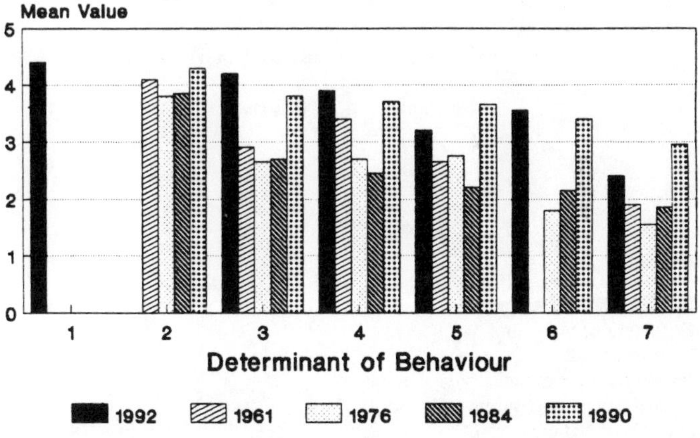

Key to Factors:

1 = Moral climate of Agency
2 = Behaviour of Superiors
3 = Behaviour of Peers
4 = Ethical practices of industry/profession
5 = Formal company/government policy
6 = Society's moral climate
7 = Personal financial need

A bar graph Figure 5.33 comparing the two Western Australian studies alone show that in three of the five instances where comparisons can be made, public sector mean values exceed those of the private sector.

In all of these comparisons both the public and the private sector in Western Australia compare very favourably with their American

Figure 5.33: Public/Private Sector Comparison (Western Australia)

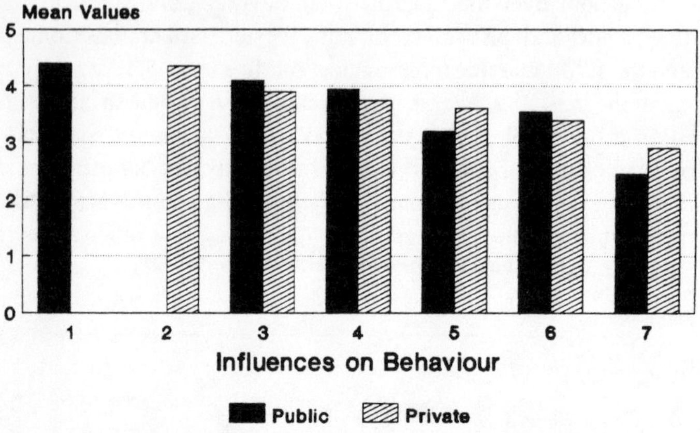

Key to Factors:

1 = Moral climate of Agency
2 = Behaviour of Superiors
3 = Behaviour of Peers
4= Ethical practices of industry/profession
5 = Formal company/government policy
6 = Society's moral climate
7 = Personal financial need

counterparts, while the Western Australian public sector produced a particularly good result by both international and local standards. When the circumstances under which the Western Australian survey was held are considered, that is the tail end of the *WA Inc* debacle, the result is both remarkable and encouraging.

Conclusions

It has been the intention of this analysis to take account only of the raw scores not the cross-tabulations of the survey and to focus primarily on the written answers of respondents. On this basis it can be deduced that so far as ethical behaviour is concerned Western Australia has a Senior Executive Service which has a well-developed sense of superiority, believing that while its ethical standards have declined somewhat in recent times they still exceed those of both the private sector – of whose ethical values they are derisive – and the community generally. This is not an unexpected finding for the senior members of a west European style public bureaucracy. Respondents rate ethics and integrity highly among their primary job skills, are reluctant to "blow the whistle" on unethical practices and almost one third of their number are aware of pressures to compromise their personal ethics to agency standards. With some this pressure to conform is increasing. Few regard good ethical practice merely as a form of rule following behaviour with technique-like characteristics but prefer a world where intangibles, such as trust, honesty and integrity count for much. Thus, they view codes of conduct as being generally ineffective. They have relatively little direct personal experience of unethical practices in their workplace but are aware of serious malpractices in the wider public sector. In both cases, patronage, in terms of "jobs for the boys", rates as the most significant.

Respondents acknowledged that unethical practice does not only result from the behaviour of individuals but, at times, from the corruption of rigorous decision-making processes. This is a relatively unexplored field. Many suggestions were made on how to reduce problems of an ethical nature in the public sector, including the use of ethics panels, the setting up of an ethics Ombudsman, the signing of ethics commitments and greater protection for whistle blowers.

Yet, in this same context their work environment provides no recognised and worthwhile support system for those facing ethical dilemmas and is instead infused with a mixture of trust and mistrust of colleagues, senior officials and "the system". Despite this they claim they would give frank and fearless advice to a minister, warning him/her if an intended course of action presented an ethical problem; many would refuse to carry out the required action even if instructed a second time. There is, on the other hand, wide disparity of opinion as to whom or what they serve; the minister, parliament, the public or whatever. This makes questions of accountability difficult to address. In the wider context there is evidence of some bitterness and cynicism at what happened to the public service under Labor in the 1980s and what they regard as the decline in traditional standards such as duty, obligation, and loyalty, as well as a blurring of the distinction between bureaucrats and politicians.

In estimating the authority and validity that should be attached to these responses the considerable experience of respondents should be taken into consideration. For example, a number of questions in the survey asked respondents to reflect upon their experience in the public sector for periods ranging from five years to the whole of their career. Given that the average respondent had worked for 3.5 public sector agencies over a period of 21 years and that more than 60% also had an average of eight years experience in the private sector, the survey was tapping into a significant time span of relevant professional experience. Thus, the survey is more than a simple snapshot in time from which little can be extrapolated either way; on the contrary, when seniority, maturity of judgement and the level of education and experience of respondents is taken into account their responses acquire significant weight.

It is necessary to make this point not only in relation to the above findings but in relation to what were the more dramatic findings of the survey, those relating to ministerial advisers. It is not intended to regurgitate the findings of questions 5, 30, 32 and 35, in particular, but it is clear that ministerial advisers were *generally* viewed by respondents as being the largest single influence responsible for a significant decline in government's ethical standards from 1983 onwards and, as a result, much of what occurred under the label of *WA Inc.* This will no doubt be regarded as a harsh judgement in the view of some, and in a sense they are right. For the political adeptness of Labor's day-to-day strategies both inside and outside the parliament could surely not have prevailed had it not been for some advisers who were equal to the best. Unfortunately, a few were probably corrupted by the political process as they became indistinguishable from ministers, while others were sucked into the vortex of "doing deals", often with a view to saving the skin of a minister who had made an incompetent yet critical decision. It was perhaps a combination of this calamitous situation together with the more brittle inter-personal encounters between ministerial advisers and members of the SES that forged the findings of this survey.

At this point it is also worth referring to a finding in a separate statistical analysis of this same survey referred to at the start of this chapter. That analysis offered no statistical support for the view that those beginning employment in the public service post 1984 adversely affected the ethical decision-making frameworks of other senior managers.(Peachment et al 1993, 16) This finding resulted from the testing of an hypothesis aimed at determining the influence of the Burke government's recruitment policies into the senior public service. While this statistical finding must stand the results of the broad brush qualitative analysis presented in these several chapters, including the findings of the royal commission, make clear that former Premier Burke cannot avoid blame for what was his key role in the recruitment and use of advisers and all that flowed from that policy.

Another finding of the earlier statistical analysis is that Senior Executive Service managers apply ethical frameworks in order to understand the meaning of "ethical behaviour" and that there are groups of managers, roughly equal in number, with distinct understandings of what constitutes ethical behaviour which is reflective of particular ethics theories. Three groups of managers are identified: (i) emphasises teleology, that is ends above means. Members of this group considered making decisions taking account of their long-term effects on society and the rights, goals and interests of others to be the most important requirements. This group felt most pressure to compromise their personal ethics and conform to agency expectations. (ii) focuses on external influences (rules, standards and codes). This group had a relatively simplistic and unelaborated understanding of ethical behaviour and held the strongest opinions about the frequency of ethical malpractice in the public sector. (iii) encompasses both teleology and external influences and, to a lesser extent deontology (means over ends). This group included public sector employees who were employed by the public service prior to 1964 and had an elaborated understanding of ethical behaviour which incorporated several theoretical perspectives. They reported little pressure to conform to organisational expectations and low instances of conflict between their personal ethics and the requirements of their agencies. They viewed society's moral climate as a critical factor and believed that public servants were aware of the *Code of Conduct*. Only this latter group is regarded as having an appropriate repertoire of potential responses to any given ethical dilemma.

One reason for undertaking the above discussion is that several (now former) ministerial advisers and one former senior minister have expressed doubts about the integrity of the questionnaire and have suggested that it unfairly "targetted" ministerial advisers. The charge is of course fatuous as, in the first place, by far the greatest amount of comment on ministerial advisers was given in response to open-ended questions which did not specifically mention them. The ferocity of the criticism levelled against them was in many ways unexpected, at least so far as the researchers were concerned. In the second place, had they been targetted, then for reasons given above SES respondents would have recognised the bias and reacted accordingly by criticising the survey. None did.

While charges of bias can be dismissed, those who believe that the judgements made against ministerial advisers are too harsh may suggest that one reason why the comments were so hostile was more a reflection of the fact that advisers had been both the initiating and driving force behind many of the reforms imposed on the service during the Burke-Dowding years, and that this was simply the reaction of conservative senior managers. That the advisers played such a leading role, particularly in the early years is probably correct. However, given the varied quality of implementation of the reforms in question it is arguably the case that far from it being the members of the SES who may have resented the reforms in question, it was the lack of knowledge of reform implementation on the part of those advisers who promoted them that was more at fault. None of this is to deny that there would certainly have been reactionary elements within the bureaucracy who would have attempted to stifle the reform process. Winning over these individuals was not aided by the Maoist approach of continuous revolution which accompanied much of the reform process. On the other hand, and more speculatively, it is suggested that responsibility may have been shared for, had questions been asked about the role and impact of international management consultants in the reform process the response may well have been comparable to that given on advisers in this survey. Unfortunately, this was a missed opportunity.

Taking all of the above into account, when respondents were asked (QUESTION 25) if unethical behaviour was a problem in the public sector the mean score was 2.7 on a five point scale. This might appear a surprisingly mild response under the circumstances for, while many of the more worrying answers given to questions may not contradict this score, it is not plausible for the many highly adverse comments about ministerial advisers to endorse this result. The explanation for this apparent dissonance in responses may result from respondents not counting ministerial advisers as part of either the public service or the public sector. Advisers were recruited from both within and outside the public sector and some became public servants (often very senior) and some did not. It is suggested that those who were parachuted into or fast-tracked through the ranks were seen as by-passing the merit system and were not widely accepted in their new role. Observations of incompetence were widely noted in others.

So as to remove any misapprehension concerning my own views on ministerial advisers it should also be made clear that there are strong arguments not only for their introduction but for their retention, and indeed upgrading within the broader framework of government. However, the excessive focus on management rather than policy related skills during the course of the Burke-Dowding years, apart from a few throw away statements, was one of the reform processes greatest weaknesses. It was clear from the results of the survey that SES members understood the checklist of factors (QUESTION 33) which related to the role of ministerial advisers, but this is far from providing an understanding of the operational and professional context within which ministerial advisers should be recruited and appointed in the national and international context of modern government. Many respondents to this survey believed that the system, whatever its advantages, was widely abused and, *WA Inc* aside, reduced the overall quality of government.

This apparent failure on the part of ministerial advisers to acquire legitimation was no doubt due to a range of factors, including the fact that while there have always been advisers in the system (Black & Peachment 1982), the lack of explanation regarding their sudden upsurge in numbers as from 1983 was unexplained. In addition there was the bad press inevitably given to advisers, in some cases deservedly so, and their intense, indeed paranoid desire for anonymity. Their failure to answer the questionnaire, for example, may well have been brought about by the fact that the questionnaire was dispatched in bundles for relevant individuals to distribute, thus, only a handful of individuals may have been responsible for the poor response. Whatever the reason it is difficult to be balanced in making judgements on individuals who come under such intense criticism and yet spurn the opportunity to offer an opinion.

References

Baxter KP (1991). "Politicisation – Responsiveness" *AJPA* 50(3) 279-83.

Black DW and Peachment A (1982). *Values and Votes: The 1980 Western Australian Election.* WA Institute of Technology.

Brannen J (ed) (1992). *Mixing Methods: Qualitative and Quantitative Research*, Aldershot, Ashgate.

Bryman in Brannen, op cit.

Campbell DT and Fiske DW (1959). "Convergent and Discriminant Validation by the Multitrait-Multimethod Matrix". *Psychological Bulletin*, 59 81-105.

Chapman RA (1988): *Ethics in the British Civil Service*, London, Routledge.

Davidow B and Williams J (1993). "Enhancing the Ethical Culture: The Approach Adopted by the Roads and Traffic Authority of New South Wales" *AJPA* 52(4) 376-82.

Denhardt KG (1991). "Ethics and Fuzzy Worlds" *AJPA* 50(3) 274-78.

Lewis PV (1985). "Defining Business Ethics: Like Nailing Jello to a Wall" *Journal of Business Ethics.* Pp 377-83.

Peachment A et al (1994). "Means or Ends?: Ethical Decision Frameworks in the Western Australian Senior Executive Service". *J Bus Ethics* (forthcoming); *Discussion Paper*, Public Sector Research Unit, Curtin Business School, 1993.

Rights, Responsibilities and Obligations: A Code of Conduct for Public Servants. Public Service Commission. Perth (1988).

Smith HR and Carroll AB (1984). "Organisational Ethics: A Stacked Deck". *J Bus Ethics* May v 3 95-100.

Soutar GN et al 1991. "The Status of Business Ethics in Perth, Western Australia". *Unpublished Research Dissertation* School of Management, Curtin University, Perth.

Topping J (1969): *Errors of Observation and Their Treatment*, London, Chapman & Hall.

Uhr J (1991). "The Ethics Debate: Five Framework Propositions". *AJPA* 50(3) 285-91.

6

From the Westminster Model to Westminster Inc

A Survey of Three States

Allan Peachment, Ian Radbone and Jean Holmes

The Westminster concept of government

The title of this book suggests that something happened to the "Westminster model" over the past decade in the three Australian States examined here. The suffix "Inc" after Westminster suggests that the model has become "incorporated" in the way a business may as each of the three governments developed significant variations from the older model, variations which while differing in important aspects also had some common origins and equally common disastrous outcomes. What the Westminster model became in each State and why requires a brief outline of the parameters that constitute the conventional model.

The concept of the "Westminster model" is of relatively recent origin, coming into common usage in Australia only in the late 1950s. It was a useful shorthand way of describing the British based system of government adapted by the Australian colonies when they set up self-governing institutions last century. It is usually taken to mean a system where:

- the head of state is not the effective head of government
- the effective head of government is a prime minister presiding over a cabinet composed of ministers over whose appointment and removal he has at least a substantial measure of control
- the executive branch of government is composed of members of the legislature

- ministers are collectively and individually responsible to a freely elected and representative legislature.

de Smith, 1961 2-16

Others have argued that in Australia it is more accurate to talk of a "Westminister syndrome" meaning:

- the doctrine of ministerial responsibility
- an official bureaucracy distinct from the political ministers and other parliamentarians
- the conviction that the elected minister should have the last word and officials must accept that
- lines of accountability running from the lowliest official up through the minister to cabinet, to the parliament, and ultimately — and only by this most circuitous and tenuous route — to the elector.

Parker, 1978 352-54

Other commentators have drawn attention to the disarming likenesses of ceremony, symbols and seating between Westminster and the Australian parliaments as well as the advantages for the executive built into the parliamentary processes and procedures. (Reid 1973; Collins 1978, 363) A recent version of the model is known as the "Washminister Mutation" which envisages a hybrid of cross-fertilised ideas taken from both Westminster and Washington. This version acknowledges increased American influence in Australia's governmental arrangements (in addition to the federal system of course) taken nowadays to include private sector style managerialism and a more empathetic advisory support structure for ministers reminiscent of White House advisers.

Whichever variation of the model is relevant, when a political party wins office in Australia it gains only limited access to political power in comparison with a British Westminster government. Constitutional constraints, High Court judgments, federal fiscal dominance, and opposing party majorities in companion governing institutions blur the authority and impact of government in Australia at all levels. Lines of accountability are also weakened when the duties and responsibilities of cabinets, parliamentarians and public officials are correspondingly nebulous and unspecified. The convention of who is responsible and accountable to whom, for what, and how often becomes almost meaningless in the Australian context. The complexities of the federal system are such that ministers and parliamentarians no longer appear to feel responsible for their actions either to parliament or to the electorate. Westminster sanctions have little meaning in a party system where strong executives are supported without criticism in legislatures dominated by loyal party majorities.

This raises the question of what constitutes the parameters of political roles at the State level in Australia today. These three late 1980s case studies suggest that considerable redefinition of the Westminster model/ syndrome/mutation is necessary if we are to prevent a repetition of the financial disasters that rocked each of the three States over the past decade.

Whether measured by political incompetence, economic mismanagement, ideological myopia and over optimism, improper and/or corrupt behaviour, sheer bad luck, or a combination of all of these and more, for the three Australian State governments surveyed here, the late 1980s were a financial and political disaster. Other State governments had undergone major trauma in the same decade on matters such as alleged political corruption, but with these the timing, nature and outcome of events all differed. Given the similarity in the outcome of their political fortunes, the three governments surveyed here are often bundled together as a kind of "gang of three", and certainly all three were understandably dismissed at the ballot box in due course. In the circumstances each State opposition needed to promise little more than retribution and an effort to clear-up the mess in order to win office. These electoral outcomes did not augur well for the ability of the electorate to hold the incoming governments accountable later.

In all three States there appears to have been a disregard for the conventions of responsibility central to the broad Westminster model and a corruption of key values, confirming Parker's conclusion, above, that the concept of Westminster has little substance in Australia. The findings and recommendations of a battalion of costly royal commissions into these events frustrated and disappointed many. The Cain government in Victoria was exonerated from legal responsibility for the failure of the State Bank's merchant subsidiary, Tricontinental, while much the same occurred in South Australia in relation to its State Bank of South Australia. Why no member of the respective governments was held responsible or prosecuted baffled many to whom the distinction between legal accountability and political responsibility made by the two Royal Commissions was meaningless. The mood was that if the system was not going to deliver up legitimate culprits then scapegoats needed to be found.[1]

---

1 Both the Victorian and the South Australian governments launched civil action against the auditors (KPMG) for providing inadequate and inappropriate audit opinions. For the Kennett government this resulted in a $136 million out of court settlement. The Brown government is claiming $3.108 billion in compensation.

In Western Australia the Royal Commissioners did blame previous Labor governments, among other factors, but even there only a handful of prosecutions of senior public servants on *WA Inc* related charges are continuing. The dramatic trials of the leading figures of the day, including two former Premiers, a former deputy Premier and several well known entrepreneurs are also continuing but on matters which fail to address the critical issues of *WA Inc*, although they do say a great deal about the standards and ethics of the time.

Significantly, whatever the various Royal Commissions reported on these matters, the former Opposition parties have in each State consistently and predictably sheeted home the blame to the three Australian Labor Party branches. This is to say that the financial disasters of the 1980s have been subsumed into the characteristic pattern of party conflict that shapes Australian government. There is much political advantage in this position of course for it infers, and in the case of Western Australia has been made explicit, that there is nothing much amiss with our political institutions and processes; now that the individuals responsible are gone from office and a few reforms of the public service have been undertaken, it can be government business as usual.

There are considerable difficulties in attempting a comparison between the three States in question over the period, but some similarities do emerge from each State's experience. All three States have an historical legacy of government intervention, often successful, as a means of restoring economic prosperity. But in Victoria the adverse outcome of the ideologically motivated Cain/Kirner governments' interventionist policies was as much the failure of the idiosyncratic corporatist strategies it used to pursue its policies as of the factors blamed by its leaders. (Cain, 1992, Ch 18) Westminster with its emphasis on the collective and individual responsibility offers no defence against the combination of bottom line accounting and socialist principles that prevailed in Victoria. If those in power do not acknowledge their responsibility, Westminster style arrangements have no sanctions.

In both South Australia and Western Australia it was again Westminster-style institutions that failed. The institutional focus in South Australia is solely on the State Bank of South Australia and the failure by political leaders to exercise the normal monitoring and control expected of an owner, whether in the private or the public sector. The Bannon government proved itself to be as inadequate a business manager as Victorian Labor. The main players in the financial tragedy that befell the State Bank of South Australia were generally honest politicians and ethical, or at least not corrupt, officials. Simple honest incompetence was to prove disastrous to the State's finances.

The Burke government in Western Australia also set out to re-align old government business enterprises and create new ones just as the Victorians and South Australians had done. Additionally there were a host of government deals with "rich mates" which later gave rise to a reciprocity where the government undertook financial rescues of its rich mates and the rich mates undertook political rescues of the government with large donations at election time. The role of the elector via the parliament was largely irrelevant and Westminster conventions appeared to have little meaning in the WA context. In terms of the damage it did to the State's economy, the privately owned Rothwells merchant bank may be taken as the equivalent of the Victorian Tricontinental and the State Bank of South Australia. Rothwells became insolvent but all three sought to bolster their liquidity by obtaining very significant government backing. Relevant additional factors in the Western Australian context were the appointment of large numbers of ministerial advisers throughout government and their widespread and negative impact on ethical values and decision making within the public service. When the research findings (Ch 5) are added to the findings by the WA Royal Commission of improper conduct on the part of some senior Labor ministers and their advisers it would appear that WA Labor made a mockery of Westminster conventions of responsibility and the strong party system rode roughshod then, as it still does, over its precepts.[2]

Most attention in these events focuses on the enormous financial losses incurred. Figure 6.1 shows that whether expressed as a total loss for the State, or as a loss incurred per head of population, South Australia is in by far the more serious position and, given that the total losses may be somewhat less than $1500m, Western Australia the least serious.[3]

2 In a survey of approximately 550 level 4-8 WA public servants held in early 1994 the question was asked: "In the time since the 1993 state election to what extent has the standard of ethics changed in your department?" The response given on a five point scale indicated that ethical standards were perceived to have marginally declined. (publication forthcoming)

3 There is difficulty in estimating Western Australia's total financial losses. For example, in December 1993, Premier Court announced that while the cost to taxpayers of the failed PICL project had blown out from $336m to $401m, the State government had settled the former Bond Corporation's $960m damages claim for $7m. (*West Australian*, 9 and 10 December 1993) For purposes of estimating the debt per head of population it should be noted that in 1991 the State's population was reported to be 1,588,000.

Figure 6.1: Total Financial Losses per State and per Head of Population

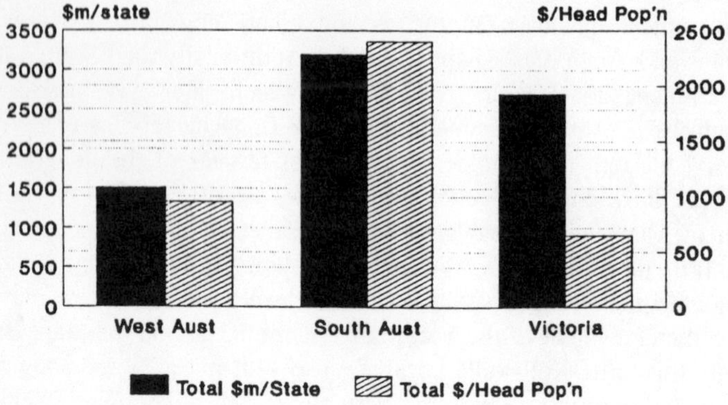

Source: See relevant chapters

The debt positions of each of the Australian States are not easily and directly comparable, but overseas ratings agencies have calculated an interstate comparison of public sector net debt for 1992. This is shown in Figure 6.2.

Figure 6.2: Public Sector Net Debt as percentage of Gross State Puoduct

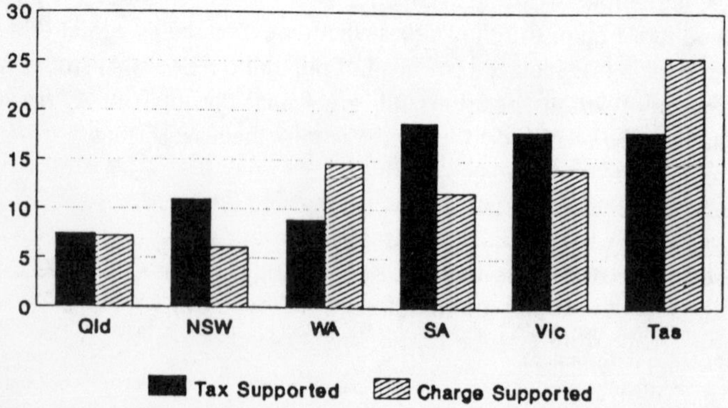

Source: S&P - Australian Ratings. 12/92

This portrays the losses in bar graph form as part of an overall percentage of Gross State Debt (GSD) expressed as (i) tax supported debt and (ii) charge supported debt. The picture now changes with Victoria displacing South Australia with an overall debt position marginally the least favourable of the three States. Western Australia retains its least serious position.

Western Australia's position is assisted by the State having had the nation's fastest growth rate over the past decade and, in theory, it should be able to pay off its debt more quickly than either of the other two States. The Kennett government in Victoria has also focused on debt reduction since it was elected in 1992, and has managed to reduce Victoria's 1993-94 deficit by $2.4 billion. (*West Australian* 27.4.94)[4]

The various Royal Commissions which looked into these matters were also costly. In Victoria the Tricontinental inquiry set up in September 1990 and reporting first in July 1991 and finally in September 1992 just before the election, cost approximately $30 million. The South Australian Royal Commission was established in March 1991, issued its first report in November 1992 and its second in September 1993 at a total cost of $30m. The Auditor-General's report which was required as part of the terms of reference was also delivered. The Royal Commission into *WA Inc* began hearings in March 1991. Part 1, six volumes, was issued in October 1992 and Part II, one volume, in November 1992 a few months before the State election. A confidential report was sent to the Director for Public Prosecutions.[5] The total cost of this inquiry, including the defence fees of government ministers and senior public servants appearing before it, was in excess of $30 million.

But financial losses were only part of the problem. The failure of State parliamentarians to hold their respective party executives to account also underlined the weakness of Westminster conventions in a strong party system. In Victoria the State's Auditor-General was often impeded in gaining proper access to some official files and his criticisms of the government's financial policies passed unheeded. In South Australia, the disinterest of MPs in accountability was demonstrated by a six year famine of Hansard references to the State Bank, of South Australia – when they eventually became interested, commercial freedom was balanced against political accountability and the former weighed more heavily. In Western

4 The Kennett government has made considerable inroads into the operating costs of public transport, for example, and about 30,000 employees have been removed from the payroll (through separation packages).

5 In 1995 the new State Attorney-General, Cheryl Edwards, instructed the Director of Public Prosecutions to give her this confidential report. Initially, the DPP refused but eventually acceded to her instruction. The report was discussed in cabinet.

Australia the new Labor Premier, Carmen Lawrence, insisted on resignations from Burke cabinet ministers Dowding, Parker and Grill, but this was more a function of political party peer group survival skills than the consequence of Westminster conventions of ministerial responsibility in operation.[6]

It was not only the political institutions that failed. The media, particularly that which is State based, was also blind to the direction in which events were moving. The South Australian media even made heroes of prominent local entrepreneurs as did the media in Western Australia, praise which only reinforced parochial attitudes towards financial dominance by the eastern States. The national media was only a little less myopic. The editor of *West Australian* has admitted to not living up to expectations during this period but has pointed out that:

> While the public may have read many of the stories, they did not hear the thousands of questions which were parried, deflected or on many occasions answered with a direct lie. They did not read the many reports which were not published when editors decided they could not be defended in law because a strong factual base could not be established, no matter how evident the wrong doing.
>
> Murray, 1991, 2

These comments must be weighed against those of former WA Deputy-Premier David Parker who said during a radio interview:

> I feel extraordinary sympathy for it (the Cain government), particularly in the last few days when I have read and heard the self-same people who have berated the Burke and Dowding governments in this state for what they did in relation to both Teachers Credit and to Rothwells and to Swan Building Society . . . those self-same people and columnists . . . getting stuck into us over that were also writing similar columns berating the Cain government for not doing what we did in relation to Pyramid
>
> David Parker (former WA Deputy Premier)
> Quoted in Peachment, 1991, 215

An interesting angle on evaluating the role of the media was the quote (allegedly made by former senator Fred Chaney), that *WA Inc* was like *Watergate* without *The Washington Post.* Chaney was correct; there were times when the media did little and other times, later, when it may have overreacted. This was particularly the case in Western Australia.[7] Others,

---

6 For an interesting analysis of the Western Australian events see McMahon, 1991.

7 Years later in July 1994 Premier Court wrote a strong protest to the editor of *West Australian* for its attempts "to re-write history" and its frequent attacks on his government. The editor responded, "Mr Court seems to think that all the problems with accountability of government ended at the election when Labor was defeated". In South

including academics and other professionals voiced little criticism. The exception in Western Australia was Professor Patrick O'Brien who:

> [W]as one of the first to blow the whistle on *WA Inc.* By talking and writing at length in the media, marching, protesting and publishing books, by withstanding scorn and ridicule which was often politically directed, he helped ensure that those connected with the state's greatest political and economic disaster are today being asked by Royal Commissioners to explain themselves.
>
> Peachment, 1992, 137

Further comparisons provide fascinating, even uncanny results. One example is the comparison between the Victorian and South Australian Royal Commission reports.

The first report of the Royal Commission into the Tricontinental Group of Companies was published months before the first report of the South Australian Royal Commission. South Australians could be forgiven for thinking that their government could have saved itself a considerable sum by simply plagiarising the Tricontinental Report, substituting Tim Marcus Clark for Ian Johns and State Bank for Tricontinental! Although only Johns was convicted of a criminal offence, the key characteristics – blind optimism, inadequate controls and accountability, arrogant disregard for sound banking practices, hero worship by the media – were all common to both States; indeed, to all three.

Yet, the two reports were dealing with significantly different problems for, during the Bannon years, South Australia's State debt was in fact decreasing while, in Victoria, Tricontinental debts were only the last straw to a State budget already overburdened by Labor's excessive borrowing to fund its Keynesian pump priming, its social justice policies and the public sector unions escalating wage demands. Public expenditure had grown more rapidly in Victoria than in the other States, and the increase in Victorian public tax revenue for 1982-83 was the highest in Australia at that time when company profits were falling. Current account expenditure was also higher as the government sought to meet the cost of the extra 9,000 plus public servants employed in the Cain government's first year in office. Net debt charges were estimated to increase nearly 40% in 1983-84. (Vic PD 1 December 1983, 2599)

This situation differs significantly from South Australia where, instead of being a key factor shaping public policy in the State, the Labor

---

Australia, Walkley Award winning journalist, Mike McEwen, was sacked from the *Advertiser* for allegedly publicly disagreeing with the Brown government's views on an Audit Commission report.(*Adelaide Review*, June 1994)

Party came to resemble the Liberal party, that is, it was little more than a vehicle for selecting candidates for parliament and helping to see that those selected were electorally successful. Unlike Victoria, party ideology and factional interests of Labor supporters played little part in South Australia. The branch has been notable for its consensus style of operation in the past (Stokes, 1983, 132-34), but while this style assisted the party's public image, it had the deleterious effect of neutering the party as a policy making body. Factions became more important in the 1980s, but a chronicler of this period has noted how rarely factional disputes hinged on policy matters, unlike Victoria. (Marshall 1992, 42) Indeed it is remarkable how little the ALP features in any of the policy histories of the years. (Parkin & Patience 1992) On the rare occasions when party policy is referred to, it is usually to indicate its vague nature or the fact that it was easily overridden or ignored.

In the early half of the 1980s the Left gained ascendancy in the South Australian ALP organisational wing, but to little practical effect and it was later replaced by the Centre Left which was dominated by parliamentarians. Party policy did provide some restraint over the development of Roxby Downs (when the Liberal Party was in government but Labor and the Democrats controlled the upper house) and, nine years later, when the government wanted to modify the Workcover scheme. On both occasions clever, if cynical, parliamentary action freed the government from the restraint and demonstrated its overwhelming concern to put office ahead of policy.

Thus, the South Australian government was free to pursue its policy inclinations of frugal, generally cautious government, steadily reducing government debt until 1990. The Cain government's financial problems appear to have arisen primarily from its preoccupation with its expansionary social justice ideology in its second term, whereas the Bannon government by contrast was criticised for its lack of vision and a fatal reliance on the expertise of managers from the private sector. (Patience 1992; Kenny 1993)

The Failure of Accountability[8]

Both the State Bank of South Australia and the State Bank of Victoria were statutory corporations, and while their status was that of financially and administratively independent government agencies, Westminster conventions of responsibility still applied to their overall activities; the government of the day is ultimately responsible for the operations of its statutory corporations. Although Rothwells was a private bank, the W.A. State government bailed it out of its financial difficulties on several occasions, and the Victorian government eventually paid out $1.3 billion for the 1991 failure of the private Pyramid building society in which many small depositors lost their savings. But in the end, whether the status of the three banks was public or private each government failed to control their financial excesses, each of their subsequent financial losses became a charge on the three States' budgets, and, with the exception of Bannon, no cabinet minister resigned as a direct consequence. Westminster syndrome conventions of responsibility and accountability had proved to be completely ineffective as a means of controlling entrepreneurial State governments. For example, the South Australian parliament was denied information about the Bank's activities on the grounds of commercial confidentiality. Premier and Treasurer John Bannon chose to be no better informed about its financial health than his Western Australian counterpart, Peter Dowding was about Rothwells – a private bank. The S.A. Auditor-General was little better placed, although he did record his criticism of three major reports from external auditors. It subsequently transpired that the South Australian State Bank's records were almost as inadequate as those of Rothwells.

Even watchdogs in the form of international and domestic accounting firms gave high credit rating or favourable auditing to the three banks in highly questionable circumstances. Nor was the role of the Australian Reserve Bank clear in all this; the Bank appeared to see its brief in relation to public financial institutions as one of monitoring the situation. At the same time, others assumed that if it did not speak out, then all was well.

In all three instances aggressive post-deregulation competition for business and a "get big or get out" mentality viewed unwise investments as counter-cyclical and therefore welcome, at least during the downturn. This short-sighted policy encouraged borrowings from reckless customers

---

8 For a recent and comprehensive account of accountability which relates to issues discussed here see Elizabeth Harman, "Accountability and Challenges for Australian Governments" *AJPA* (1994) vol 29 pp 1-17.

and none of the three State Premiers recognised the pitfalls for their governments in this high risk – high growth/profit corporate lending policy. The overlaying of this with a private sector style managerialism in the case of Tricontinental and the State Bank meant that, in comparison with Rothwells, there was no important difference between the three banks in terms of financial accountability nor in the potentially disastrous outcomes for the public and the private sectors.

Ministers and Their Staff

At this point the contrasts between Western Australia and the other two States becomes evident. In Western Australia some ministers and their staff actively pursued their interests in a way which corrupted the government's relationship with the financial sector, but in South Australia the political role regarding the State Bank was characterised by naivety and neglect. In Victoria the Cain government appeared to have something of a distaste for the profit orientation of the commercial arm of its State Bank. The remedies that flowed from the respective Royal Commission inquiries reflected these differences.

In South Australia inadequate monitoring and assessment of the Bank was seen as a cause of the disaster. Consequently the Treasury has now been granted its wish of having a representative on the Board of the Bank. Compare this with the situation in Western Australia where it was argued that senior public servants (former ministerial advisers) should have no say in the management of a public enterprise. To quote the Royal Commission:

> If a measure of independence is so given, it is wholly inappropriate that a public servant be appointed to the board of that body while retaining his or her position in the Public Service in a Department within any portfolio of the minister responsible for that body . . .. It is quite improper for public servants to be put in a position where they are expected to serve two masters, no matter how honest and well-intentioned the individuals concerned may be. The inevitable conflicts created by such appointments discredit the autonomy the body is intended to have.
>
> RC 3.14.12(d)

The middle ground between having inadequate monitoring and that of appointing watchdogs with a conflict of interests may be one with as many dangers as these two alternatives.

The Victorian outcome was equally idiosyncratic. The Commission's report exonerated the government from any blame for the Tricontinental disaster, and the new premier, Joan Kirner, was quick to capitalise on this finding in her subsequent election campaign. The party maintained its distance from the commercial financial world to the end, but it was forced to sell the parent State Bank of Victoria to the Commonwealth Bank of Australia to defray the Tricontinental debts.

But perhaps the most interesting contrast concerns ethics. Whereas ethics was a key issue in Western Australia with many prominent individuals being found to have behaved improperly (Chapter 4), in South Australia where the Bank losses were much larger, no one has been charged. The losses were ascribed to simple honest incompetence by Bank executives with the Royal Commission concluding that there were "no instances" of fraudulent and dishonest behaviour by the Bank's directors or officials. (*Advertiser,* 8 September 1993, 1) In Victoria the Bank's managing director and 1986 Young Executive of the Year, Ian Johns, served a short goal sentence for accepting commissions on loans. He was ordered to repay $1.9 million and was later declared bankrupt.[9]

Other cases of questionable ethics included conflicts of interest of senior executives in relation to making loans, frequent cases of passing misleading information to both the Bank Board and to Premier Bannon, and the use of a Cayman Islands tax haven.[10]

Though John Bannon quite rightly took the political blame for the State Bank losses, it has not been suggested that his behaviour was illegal or dishonest, nor that it was motivated in any way by personal greed. Bannon had the reputation of being frugal and materially modest. Kenny has argued that it was Bannon's otherworldly attitude to money that ill-fitted him for his responsibilities to oversee the State's commercial activities. "The paradox left behind – a stingy premier becoming our most costly – suggests that he is a man for whom money is a bit of a mystery". (Kenny 1993, 112) Nor were Premiers Burke, Dowding or Cain flamboyant characters in a material sense. During his term of office Burke lived in a working class suburb surrounded by family.

---

9 On 13 July 1994 former premier Burke was sentenced to two years' jail for defrauding the State by claiming a total of $17,000 from his travel allowance to which he was not entitled.

10 Readers will of course recognise parallels between this and everyday behaviour among some of (Western) Australia's more notable entrepreneurs. For example, in May 1994, it was revealed that within days of the $370m government rescue of his merchant bank, which followed the stock market crash of October 1987, Laurie Connell began moves to protect the family properties valued at $3.1m to put them out of reach of creditors. (*West Australian,* 10 May 1994)

In a strategic sense, from its earliest days in office the Burke government:

> [S]ought to mould the machinery of government to reflect its priorities and particular concerns. (This involved), most obviously, the appointment of a considerable cadre of party-sympathizers to ministerial staffs, significant recruitment at senior levels in those departments servicing priority policy areas and changes to the structure of the bureaucracy designed to emphasise and provide resources for its major areas of commitment.
>
> Forrest, *AJPA* XLIII(2) 1984, 156

While most of the new positions were advertised outside the service since well-qualified appointees were apparently being sought, there was much talk of stacked selection panels and jobs for the boys and girls. "Parachuting" was perceived as being of Arnhem-like proportions and as disastrous. By way of contrast, whereas many ministerial staff "parachuted" into key public service positions were regarded as a malign influence in Western Australia, the rare times that ministerial staff are mentioned in South Australia's reports indicate no malign influence. Indeed they were among the few being frank with the premier, passing on information and urging an independent inquiry into the State's banking activities. (RC First Report, 164, 253, 320)[11]

In South Australia the traditional public servants by contrast, often failed the "frank and fearless" injunction required of them under the Westminster system. Evidence suggests that this was less the case in Western Australia where, in a colourful description of an unconventional Westminster relationship, Premier Dowding was said to have flown into a rage when told by "frank and fearless" public servants (in this case former Burke appointed advisers) the extent of the growing Rothwells disaster, shouting "I am surrounded by liars and cheats". (McCusker, 331) While it was true that there was a general reluctance to play the Jeremiah, it seems the more important problem was that the seriousness of the situation – the behaviour of the financial institutions and the effect on government finances that resulted – was of an order that traditional forms of bureaucratic language were just not capable of communicating.

The Cain government introduced a coordinated system of ministerial advisers in Victoria for the explicit purpose of ensuring that ministers

---

11 On his first day as Premier-elect, South Australian Premier, Dean Brown dismissed the State's most senior public servant, Premier's Department Head, Peter Crawford. Also casualties were Under-Treasurer, Peter Emery, Health Commission Head, David Blaikie and Department of Family and Community Services Head, Anne Dunn. Other senior officers were shifted to new positions. *(West Australian* 15 December 1993). Curiously, in Western Australia the number of public servants dismissed was a mere handful.

obtained support from sources independent of the mainstream bureaucracy, that is, they were appointments in direct contradiction to Westminster conventions.[12] They were a partisan service – "able qualified advisers with both political and policy skills who were loyal to the government rather than to individual ministers". (Considine, 1992 194-96) Often they came in as advocates of party policy, and by 1987 they were fast becoming a liability to the government as political aspirants and leaders used their role as adviser to promote sectional interests. Ideological commitment had become party self-interest and the Labor government suffered accordingly. All this evidence suggests that, in all three States, the old virtue of being frank and fearless was, for a variety of reasons, lost in the new managerial regimes.[13]

The South Australian Treasury did make an effort to act in a way which it believed reflected the wishes of the minister. In a colourful description of the traditional Westminster relationship, Royal Commissioner described Treasury as the "faithful courtesan to the Treasurer's expectations of it, no more and no less". (RC, First Report, 267)

The same State provided an interesting case of an informed individual whose concerns were so serious that it led to an attempt to "blow the whistle" in a manner similar to the Ponting case (Chapter 4) by communicating with a member of parliament.[14] The Opposition spokesperson on the Bank, Jennifer Cashmore, had a "deep throat" who told her of an important loan which was not approved by loans officers, a decision that was overridden by Bank executives. However it is obvious

---

12 The following account is taken from M Considine "Labor's Approach to Policy Making" in M Considine and B Costar (eds) *Trials in Power*, MUP 1992 , 194-196.

13 In South Australia Under-Treasurer Bert Prowse was a career bureaucrat with a long career in the Commonwealth public service behind him. His gentle, elliptical form of communication was referred to by Commissioner Sam Jacobs on several occasions, at one stage referring to his "courteous nature and unprovocative personality and temperament". (RC First Report, 301) This approach was maintained even when his approaches for information and dialogue were rudely rebuffed by the Bank. As the Royal Commissioner continued:

> He was simply not prepared to rock the boat. He was at the very least highly apprehensive, if not convinced, that it was sailing into stormy waters, but he knew and was constantly reminded that the Treasurer . . . had set the course, and in the light of past experience, was unlikely to change it.
>
> RC, First Report, 301-02

14 During the early months of the Court government's term of office in 1993 there was an interesting piece of street theatre when the Premier blew the whistle on the public service by insisting on the Under-Treasurer accompanying him to face the media on the steps of Parliament to explain the nature of an alleged Treasury error.

that the informant was agonised by the ethical dilemma involved as, although encouragement was offered by Ms Cashmore, little more information was forthcoming even though she was convinced that the informant knew more.

The ethical concerns revealed by the State Bank disaster are therefore muted and subtle. But a focus on ethics in terms of individual behaviour ignores the pervading climate of financial excess that was a far more significant factor. There were signs of unethical behaviour of a systemic kind and certainly there was greed, ranging from the South Australian workers on the REMM site, who were paid an allowance not to whistle at girls walking by, to the enormous salaries and luxury perks granted to senior executives. But while the picture of finance executives engorging themselves on $300,000 plus salaries while the average employee's real pay was being shrunk by the Accord may be offensive, the greed was "legitimate" greed, sanctioned by due process and legalised by the law of supply and demand.

The South Australian community has found it hard to accept that so much money could be lost without criminal activity being involved. This simple-minded view was best expressed in an *Advertiser* editorial the day after the final royal commission report was released.

> [I]t was not good enough to say that no-one was criminally culpable. This was a wall of money. To conclude that it vanished because of "errors of judgement" and inadequacies in establishing and policing prudential policies is pathetic.

As the first royal commissioner responded, "Although there may be some public disappointment with the outcome . . . the Commission cannot be expected to create or invent offences unknown to the law." (*Advertiser,* 9 September 1993, 2)

It was the *Advertiser* editorial rather than the Royal Commission's response that best reflected the anger and frustration felt by South Australians facing a disaster so real in terms of the effects on State finances and yet so opaque in terms of its cause. A similar situation occurred in Victoria where the Royal Commissioner also found that the failings of Tricontinental's managing director, Ian Johns, were those of an "over-confident gambler, not of a criminal" and that the Bank's financial losses did not stem from the government, an over-confident bureaucracy or official or commercial corruption. They too were:

> [U]nable to point to any time when, or identify any issue where, the Treasurer failed in his administration, supervision or monitoring of SBV or its subsidiary. On the contrary, the evidence shows that, in these matters, he

> acted responsibly at all times. . . . If this is so of the former Treasurer, it is even clearer in the case of the Premier . . . the Commission finds that Mr Cain acted properly and responsibly at all times in relation to all the matters within its terms of reference.
>
> First Report of the Royal Commission into
> the Tricontinental Group of Companies
> 30 July 1991, paras 24:130;131;133

The oft asked question – *But where has all the money gone?* — is not easily answered. Some went to brand new but empty buildings, in shops that are occupied, but only at a peppercorn rent, programs begun in hope and subsequently closed down as funding disappeared, some simply cannot be traced. In a less tangible way the answer to the question is evident in the things that are not there – the schools, hospitals and homes that will not be built; the caring programs and training policies that will not be implemented, research, lower taxes and charges that will not materialise – the list is endless. In Victoria and South Australia the causal factors were the unreasoning optimism of management which was never subject to adequate checking by the banks' parliamentary owners. (Western Australia was more complicated) And for this the banks owners' – the South Australian and Victorian communities as a whole – must bear a sizable chunk of the responsibility.

Financial leadership

The questionable nature of the leadership qualities of some of the main players in the State banking disasters is also a matter for comment and speculation. Both Tricontinental and the State Bank of S.A. were government instrumentalities, but the values with which they were infused via recruitment and staffing were very much those of the private sector. Tricontinental's Ian Johns had no tertiary qualifications while the head of the S.A. State Bank, Marcus Clark, held an MBA from Harvard University. Both men were aggressively entrepreneurial by nature, and the independent status of their respective public sector organisations allowed their talents full play.

In Western Australia the story was different again. Laurie Connell, managing director of Rothwells Merchant Bank, was an unqualified self-made multi-millionaire who began his working life as a government messenger boy. But during the 1980s his relationship with government, and especially with Premier Burke, typified that of the non-traditional, new age entrepreneurs favoured by the premier. In all three cases the premiers liked the look of and placed inordinate faith in their chosen gurus – as they did with a number of other notable financial failures – in Western Australia at least.[15] But in a sense the integrity of Clark, Johns or Connell was irrelevant, and the fact that it was not the government but the board of the State Bank of Victoria who appointed Johns as Tricontinental managing director made no difference to the eventual outcome. No premier – neither Cain, Bannon, Burke nor Dowding – knew what was going on when it came to the final collapse.[16] What Guerin said about Bannon — that he was not a financier nor a top rate practical manager and that while he had a grasp of economics, he was no economist – applies to all of the premiers. Law was (and still is) the favoured discipline, not public sector management or public finance.

All four premiers strongly endorsed the importance of private sector managerial concepts and skills for public sector work at every opportunity; it took the new W.A. Labor Premier, Carmen Lawrence, to recognised what many academics had been saying for years, namely that "Experiences in Australia and overseas have demonstrated that increasing adoption of private sector practices is not the answer." But such adoptions have continued apace. (*Managing for Balance*, 1992, Preface; See Peachment 1986)

A stress on management skills in government also failed to protect the Victorian government from the partisan pressures that were to inflate the State budgets even before the Tricontinental debacle occurred. This approach was in sharp contrast to South Australia's frugality but nevertheless, the Bannon government was criticised for its overreliance on the market. This was not the case in Western Australia. For most of the period people admired Labor's tenacity, drive and vision. At the time of Burke's retirement in 1987 a Japanese investment service gave the State an AA+ credit rating, thus ranking its economic integrity ahead of that of the nation. This was based on factors which included mineral resource

---

15 It is not unfair to compare Burke with disgraced President Nixon who it is said lacked one quality of the great leader: the ability to select subordinates wisely. Len Brush and Tony Lloyd were only two of the more prominent examples noted by the Commission. (See Jonathan Aitken, *Nixon: A Life,* Weidenfeld and Nicolson, 1993)

16 One person who did claim to know of the impending disaster was then backbencher and now Premier, Richard Court. Court gave evidence to the Commission that he knew a year before the October 1987 rescue that more than half the Rothwells loans were to Connell or Connell-related companies. He claimed to have been told this in confidence by a person experienced in the banking industry who was involved in the Treasury operations at Rothwells. His informant had said that the company would collapse like a pack of cards, but Court said he did not mention this to former Premier Brian Burke during the rescue weekend. (*West Australian* 23 May 1992)

developments, goldmining and the economic impact of that "hallmark event", the America's Cup. (Peachment, 1988, 185, 187) Even as late as August 1990 the New York credit rating agency Standard and Poors gave the Western Australian government's overseas borrowing program a AA rating. Immediately beforehand, Moody's gave the State's long term currency debt obligations a AA2 rating. (*West Australian,* 1 and 7 August 1990) The fact that Labor survived the 1989 election – on some counts by a mere 160 votes – was perhaps a reflection of this mood of high public expectation.

But why?

As the events of the eighties slowly fade from the community memory, the question, why did it happen, remains largely unanswered. Why did the governments in the three States encounter similarly disastrous circumstances concurrently? Earlier chapters explain how banks collapsed, how premiers and cabinets lost control, how some senior decision makers and advisers behaved badly or stupidly and have described some of the characteristics of those involved. But this does not explain how in all three States these events could have occurred at the one time. Surely it was not just coincidence! And surely too, the emerging myth in Western Australia, and perhaps in the other States, that these financial debacles were an aberration that will not recur, is too dangerous a belief to leave unchallenged. It seems important to tease out some of the common factors and examine their relevance for the future.

The historical tension in all three States between a perceived need for industrial development and the appropriate role for parliament in a modern liberal democracy appears to be a major contextual factor. Industrial development brings with it jobs and increased government revenue, the latter providing resources for new policy initiatives and thus improved prospects of re-election. All three State governments in this period aimed to control their capital market and direct it towards the needs of State development as they saw it. In Victoria Labor set up the Victorian Economic Development Corporation to distribute resources in accordance with the government's priorities, and in Western Australia, Labor strategists first developed a similar initiative as early as 1979 when in opposition. The idea there was to overcome the problem of a State that was resource rich but capital poor and to assist economic development by better utilising lazy government assets. (Grill, 1991) Eventually a Western Australian Development Corporation was proclaimed in 1984 and the Western Australian Export Import Corporation was incorporated in 1985. (Schapper, 1993, 30) Views as to their success is divided. (Horgan, 1991) In South Australia the State Bank Act was also drafted to enable it to expand its funding activities. In effect, during this period Labor in all three States, while pursuing issues of social justice and the environment, became development junkies more so than their predecessors.

A further strand running through all of the three accounts of each State's experiences was that of federal-State financial relations or more specifically, vertical fiscal imbalance (VFI),[17] and its impact on a States' ability to exercise new policy options.[18] This factor has long been a serious problem for all the Australian States and, with the economic downturn in recent times it has been exacerbated. By comparison with other mature federations such as Canada, Germany and the United States of America VFI is severe in Australia. In 1991-92 Australia's Commonwealth government is estimated to have collected about 73% of the total own source revenue generated by all levels of government but to have spent only 52% on total own purpose expenditures. (Kerr 1993, 67) Most of the remainder is transferred conditionally to the States severely constraining the development of alternative policy options by the various State governments. (Schapper, 1993)

---

17 Vertical fiscal imbalance is defined as "the difference between own source revenue and own purpose expenditure commitments for a level of government".(WPTP, 1991 p 6)

18 Writing on this problem in Australia Kerr argues that:

> [T]he regime of state taxation in Australia is a mishmash of nuisance taxes – regressive, distortionary taxes, many of which are unpopular, are costly to administer and/or impose high compliance costs on taxpayers. The taxes levied by State Governments are mostly either taxes rejected by the Commonwealth Government or other taxes that the States have independently implemented and which have not been ruled by the High Court to be constitutionally unacceptable. These taxes are often imposed, virtually regardless of any merits or demerits they might have, merely because they are the only revenue sources available to the States.
>
> This is not to say that the States have been completely innocent victims, totally blameless for the parlous position of the State taxation structure. On the contrary, the States have shown a reluctance to exploit fully the tax bases available to them, a willingness to grant tax exemptions where there is political milage in so doing and a tendency to blame the Commonwealth Government and the extent of VFI for all their problems, including those of their own making. (Kerr 1993, 65-66)

A special Premiers' Conference Working Party Report (WPTP, 1991, 10) argued that VFI created a range of problems:

> States may not have the revenue capacity to respond in an effective and timely way to community preferences.
>
> States do not have to bear the total cost of their expenditure decisions and therefore have an incentive to overspend.
>
> State government efforts can be focussed on increasing Commonwealth grants, rather than on raising their own taxing efforts.
>
> Duplication and overlap of expenditure responsibilities between the Commonwealth and State governments is promoted.
>
> VFI and the associated system of specific purpose grants can distort both expenditure patterns and revenue decisions at all levels of government.

Immediately after the election of the Burke government in 1983, it was reported that from its earliest days in office:

> [T]he Government had been particularly conscious of the diminishing state and the Commonwealth's increasingly parsimonious view of the financial assistance that should be provided to the resource-rich states. . . . Faced with a commitment to an extensive and in many cases expensive program of reform and very real limitations on its traditional sources of revenue, the Government has sought to adopt a more entrepreneurial role itself in order to minimise the transfer of locally generated economic surpluses to the Commonwealth. In other words involvement with the private sector . . . is seen as a way of protecting the State's economic base against intrusion by the Commonwealth under the corporations power whose constitutionality was confirmed by the High Court in the Dams case.
>
> Forrest 1984, 156
>
> (See also B Burke 1984)

The premier warned of the shortcomings of Australia's federal system in his first major speech after winning the election, describing it as one of the biggest dangers facing his administration. (Peachment, 1987, 243)

In addition to VFI and its effect in starving the States of resources the effect on the Australian federal system itself is to invite different levels of government to consider adopting contrasting economic policy initiatives concurrently. The intergovernmental policy and management difficulties this arrangement creates have long been noted for:

> [D]espite some initial success, no modern Australian State government can consistently pursue economic policies when the federal government is committed to a diametrically opposite programme.
>
> Considine 1992, 1

Neither Cain in Victoria, Bannon in South Australia nor Burke and Dowding in Western Australia could be regarded as proponents of the federal governments policies of economic rationalism. When it came to constraints on their policy initiatives, all three State governments had grounds for their perception that Australia's Federal-State financial arrangements hobbled their freedom to pursue their preferred State policy options. In the resulting attempts at policy innovation some may work, for a time, others may not. Some may have moderate although often unacknowledged success in the longer term.[19]

The Western Australian Labor government also regarded the Legislative Council, the State's upper house as a serious impediment to the pursuit of its policies and others have made the same point in Victoria. (Costar 1992, 204-206)[20] Reform of both State upper houses was high on each State's Labor Party agenda in 1982-3 and important changes were eventually made, but these did not remove the coalition parties' variable influence on Labor's policy agenda. In both States there are those who would argue that the idea of a hostile upper house is a figment of Labor's imagination (for example, in Victoria the late Premier Sir Henry Bolte had a hostile upper house for most of his government's term in office). Given the lack of comprehensive evidence for either point of view differing perceptions will prevail but in both States Labor has always believed that when in office its legislative initiatives would be neutered by the upper house. This provided an added incentive for the Cain and Burke governments to adopt a strategy of negotiation and compromise and a separation of the coalition parties in the upper house to the advantage of their respective governments. (Costar 1992, 204-213) By way of contrast, since the mid-1970s South Australia's upper house (Legislative Council) has been elected on a basis of proportional representation, full franchise. As such it is more democratically elected than the House of Assembly. For

---

19 The WA Development Corporation provides such an example.

20 Costar argues that Victorian labor re-wrote the State's electoral laws by skilful bargaining.

most of that time the Australian Democrats have had the balance of power, giving it a "left wing" and pro-accountability influence.[21]

In Western Australia one strategy adopted by the Burke government to overcome this legislative threat was to enact two pieces of legislation which greatly enhanced the powers of the government to interface with and operate in the commercial sphere. This 1983 development represented a significant new phase in the interpenetration of government and business in the history of public enterprise in Western Australia. (Harman, 1986 247) The first phase, which was plagued by financial mismanagement and a lack of accountability, was the wide-ranging commercial activities pursued by the Scadden Labor government (WA) (1911-16) which was partly brought to a halt by the *State Trading Concerns Act* 1917. The second phase occurred in the 1940s and 1950s under the Labor governments of Wilcox and Hawke. This too ended in mismanagement, losses and public disenchantment. (Harman 1986, 246) Harman has argued that in the 1980s developments both the government and the opposition interacted to create hybrid enterprises which neither Australian political ideologies nor legal practice were yet equipped to handle. For instance, the new (and later notorious) parent company, Western Australian Government Holdings (WAGH) was not accountable to State parliament which was effectively by-passed.

The idea was highly innovative and in some ways successful but it was "mercilessly exploited" years later in the disastrous $175m PICL-Rothwells bailout. (Peachment, 1991, 200) This move from being progressive and enterprising in developing policy ideas to having those same ideas corrupted came about from the additional layer added to the business-government relationship. In effect it was a link between Labor leaders and selected high flying local entrepreneurs with international reputations. This was both the nub and the newsworthy aspect of *WA Inc*.

The final common factor which throws some light on the collapse in the three states analysed here is the supportive, uncritical role played by the media in all three States. In Western Australia for example relations between executive government and the media had rarely attracted such sustained interest as that applied by former journalist and Premier, Brian Burke. (Kennedy, 1991, 71) The State's monopoly newspaper, the *West Australian*, (but no TV channel) has long acknowledged criticism of its role in these critical events. In South Australia the fawning attitude of the

21 The leader of the Democrats, Ian Gilfillen, was one of two members willing to ask questions about the State Bank when it was unfashionable to do so. The Bank silenced him with threats of legal action.

press towards the former premier and Clark has gone but the savaging of critics has not entirely disappeared in relation to the current Brown government. In Victoria the Cain government established a high powered media sub-committee located in the reorganised Premier's Department. It produced an avalanche of press statements of which only a tiny fraction were either recorded or published while Opposition criticism of the government's financial policies received little coverage until late in Labor's second term. When over 100,000 Victorians assembled in a massive public rally outside parliament house calling for an immediate election the Victorian media dismissed their cry as a one day wonder.

Clearly, the three States surveyed here differed in their response to the events of the 1980s. The Western Australian outcomes are not really explained by the view that the State "retains to the present day a nineteenth buccaneering character long since displaced in the rest of the country". (Halligan & Power 1992, 255) One interesting possibility for interpreting the response of all three States is contained in research by Danemark and Sharman (1994) and their efforts to establish whether the Australian States have discernible regional political cultures. Testing nationally for efficacy, involvement and trust, these researchers found strong differences between the States regarding trust in government. They concluded that:

> When these differences were controlled for partisan and socioeconomic effects, significant differences persisted, producing three distinct categories of states. Respondents in Queensland and Western Australia had a much more favourable attitude to their state government than the federal government when compared with the federal sample overall, a pattern that was reversed for the residents of New South Wales and Victoria. The responses of South Australians and Tasmanians were close to the Australian mean, though favouring the federal government over state governments.
>
> (p 96)

The tripartite division between the States is most interesting, since it neatly separates the three States surveyed here in a way that implies a relationship between trust in State governments and the outcomes described. The possibilities are intriguing.

Despite the similarity of its financial experience in the 1980s with Victoria and South Australia, Western Australia, the State displaying most trust in its State government was also the least electorally punitive when Labor was dismissed in 1993. Victorian electors, preferring to place their trust in the federal government, penalised the Labor government heavily for incurring such massive debts and high unemployment. South Australia, while closer to the mean for trust in government, appears to have been at least as punishing in its reaction to Premier Bannon's financial disasters with Labor winning only 10 seats in the 47-seat House of Assembly.

In seeking an explanation for what happened under Labor in the 1980s in South Australia, Western Australia and Victoria, the role of fashionable ideas in reforming the public sector, most of them originating in the private sector, played out against the contextual variables outlined above is almost certainly important. The fervour for such ideas resembled a kind of private sector fundamentalism, as Keynes's well known aphorism suggests, the world appears to be driven by little else but ideas both good and bad. Schon (1971) has already asked some of the important questions concerning this process when he questioned the means by which certain ideas come into good currency and why old questions and dilemmas are frequently not answered but simply go out of fashion. The ideas which did much of the damage in terms of financial accountability and the losses incurred in each state were those which were intended to enhance business-government relations. But there were others. These three case studies suggest that the concept of the Westminster syndrome in Australian government offers an inadequate explanation for what has occurred. The political times are ripe for a new paradigm of representative and responsible government whereby a strong party executive can be held accountable for its stewardship and where it clearly understands the role of the State and the limits of that role.

References

Armstrong, H, "The Tricontinental Affair" in Considine M and Costar B (eds) (1992) *Trials in Power: Cain, Kirner and Victoria 1982-1992*, Melbourne UP, 43-58.

Burke, B (1984) "Federalism After the Franklin" *Aust Qtly* 4-9.

Cain, J (1992) "Achievements and Lessons for Reform Governments" in Considine and Costar (eds) (1992) *Trials in Power: Cain, Kirner and Victoria 1982-1992*, Melbourne UP, 265-280.

Collins, H (1978) "What Shall We Do With The Westminster Model?" in Smith RFI & Weller P (eds) (1978), *Public Service Inquiries in Australia*. St Lucia, University of Queensland Press.

Considine, M and Costar B (eds), (1992) *Trials in Power: Cain, Kirner and Victoria 1982-1992* Melbourne UP.

Costar B (1992) "Constitutional Change" in Considine M and Costar B (eds) op cit 201-214.

Denemark, D and Sharman C (1994), "Political Efficacy, Involvement and Trust: Testing for Regional Political Culture in Australia" *AJPS* vol 29 81-102.

de Smith, SA (1961) "Westminister's Export Models: The Legal Framework of Responsible Government" in *JCW Political St* 1:1, 2-16.

Forrest, M (1984) *AJPA* XLIII(2), 156-162.

Grill, J "Policy Innovation as Imagination: Political Origins of the WADC" in Peachment A (1991), *The Business of Government: Western Australia 1983-1990* (171-187) Sydney, The Federation Press.

Halligan, J and Power J (1992), *Political Management in the 1990s* Oxford UP.

Harman, E J (1986) "Government and Business in Western Australia, 1983-85: Legal and Political Aspects of the New Hybrid Enterprises" *AJPA* XLV(3) 247-62.

Harman, E J (1992) "Public and Corporate Duties: The Lloyd Case in Western Australia" *AJPA* 51(1) 86-95.

Horgan, J (1991),"The Private Sector and Government: WADC – An Agent for Change" in Peachment (1991) op cit. 1-18.

Kennedy, P (1991), "Managing the Media" in Peachment op cit 70-86.

Kenny, C (1993) *State of Denial* Adelaide, Wakefield.

Kerr, I A (1993), "Taxation Measures to Reduce Vertical Fiscal Imbalance in Australia: A Review of the October 1991 Report of the Working Party on Tax Powers" in Collins DJ (ed) *Vertical Fiscal Imbalance and the Allocation of Taxing Powers* Sydney, Australian Tax Research Foundation, 65-95

McCusker, M J (1990), "Report of an Inspector on a Special Investigation into Rothwells Ltd" (PtI) Quoted in Peachment (1991) op cit p 213.

McMahon, L *The Balance of Responsibility: Ministers, Advisors and the Senior Public Service* in Peachment (1991) op cit 129-150.

"Managing for Balance: A Public Sector Management Strategy" (1992) Government of Western Australia.

Marshall V (1992) "The Labor Party" in Parkin, A and Patience, A (eds) *The Dunstan Decade: The Politics of Restraint* Sydney, Allen & Unwin, 36-49.

Murray, P (1991), *Arming the Press to Deal With WA Inc When it Arises Next* Curtin Business Centre.

O'Brien, P (ed), (1986), *The Burke Ambush: Corporatism and Society in Western Australia* Perth, Apollo Press.

O'Brien, P and Webb, M (eds) (1991), *The Executive State: WA Inc and the Constitution* Perth, Constitutional Press.

Parkin, A and Patience, A (1992), *The Bannon Decade; the Politics of Restraint* Sydney, Allen & Unwin.

Parker, R S (1978) "The Public Service Inquiries and Responsible Government" in Smith, RFI and Weller, P (eds) *Public Service Inquiries in Australia.* St Lucia UQP 334-359.

Patience, A (1992), "The Bannon Decade: Preparation for What?" in Parkin & Patience op cit 343-54.

Peachment, A (1986), "'Management' and the 'Public Sector': Never Mind the Reality, Feel the Myth" *Can Bull Pub Admin* XIII/2 Winter, 130-37.

Peachment, A (1987) "Chronicle" *AJPA* XLVI(2), 239-244.

Peachment, A (1988) "Chronicle" *AJPA*, XLVII(2) 185-91.

Peachment, A (1991), *The Business of Government: Western Australia 1983-1990* Sydney, The Federation Press.

Peachment, A (1992), Book review of: *The Executive State: WA Inc and the Constitution* (Perth, Constitutional Press) *AJPA* 51(1) March 137-38.

Reid, GS (1973) "The Trinitarian Struggle: Party-Executive Relationships" in Mayer, H and Nelson, H (eds) *Australian Politics: A Third Reader* Melbourne, Chesire 513-526.

Schapper, P, "Commonwealth-State Financial Relations and the Policy Environment" in Peachment et al (1993), *Case Studies in Public Policy* Perth, Public Sector Research Unit 14-35.

Schon, D A (1971), *Beyond the Stable State: Public and Private Learning in a Changing Society* Pelican.

Stokes, G (1983), "South Australia: Consensus Politics" in Parkin, A and Warhurst, J (eds) *Machine Politics in the Australian Labor Party* Sydney, Allen & Unwin.

Victoria, Parliamentary Debates, 1 December 1983, 2599.

(WPTP) Working Party on Tax Powers (1991), *Taxation and the Fiscal Imbalance Between Levels of Australian Government,* Report to the 20-21 November 1991 Special Premiers's Conference.

Index